The Product Is You!

Position Yourself for Success as an Advisor

By

Mark Magnacca

COMPLIMENTS OF

GUARDIAN
INVESTOR SERVICES LLC

1-800-650-6505

ISBN: 1-4107-6367-6 (e-book)
ISBN: 1-4107-6368-4 (Paperback)

Library of Congress Control Number: 2003094273

This book is printed on acid free paper.

Printed in the United States of America
Bloomington, IN

1stBooks - rev. 10/03/03

Dedication

This book is dedicated to my wife and best friend Kristen. As my trusted advisor, she's helped me to understand what really matters. I'm grateful for her unwavering support, incredible intuition and tremendous patience.

Acknowledgements

I want to thank all my advisor-coaching clients and seminar participants who have helped me crystallize my thinking and raise my standards.

There are so many people who have gone the extra mile for me and who have helped make this journey exciting and meaningful. They have all given me something that has helped make this book possible. I am grateful to you all.

Some of these people include: Nick Corvenus, Joe Deitch, Doug Dubiel, Kent Fitzpatrick, Suzanne Foxwell, Jeff Goldberg, Jackie Herskovitz, Tony Jeary, Al Martella, Frank Maselli, Donald Moine, Ed Sierawski, Dan Sullivan and Neil Wood. This amazing group of individuals, each in their own unique way, helped me to reach a new level of performance.

My Forum One Group: Bill Kazman, Yuchun Lee, John Miller, Marty Murphy, Cris Peterson, Mario Ricciardelli, Matt Rosenthal, Eric Silverman. This "Great Group" of young entrepreneurs has inspired me every month for almost a decade with their dedication, insight and humor.

My Family…

Kristen and Cole Magnacca, I'm grateful for your unconditional support and endless encouragement. You make it all worthwhile!

Diana Truax, Robert Magnacca, Scott Magnacca, Thanks for all you have done for allowing me to make my dreams a reality.

Ginger and Lu Nehring. Thanks for your support and encouragement.

And a special tribute to the memory of my friend and mentor Richard B. Ross.

Table of Contents

Forward viii

Introduction **Why Not You?** ix

>Figuring out how to use your biggest resource – *You* – more effectively.

Chapter 1 **The Mental Thermostat:** 1

>Overcoming the obstacles *you* impose on yourself.

Chapter 2 **The Product Is You** 19

>The best thing you have to sell is *you.* How to present your most important product in the best light.

Chapter 3 **The Elevator Speech** 45

>How to quickly and effectively communicate what you do in 30 seconds or less to make a lasting impression.

Chapter 4 **Fishing Where the Fish Are** 77

>Identifying your ideal target clients and developing the best strategy to attract them.

Chapter 5 **Your Personal IPO (Initial Prospect Offering)** 99

>Packaging your process and credentializing *You* as an expert.

Chapter 6 **The Referral Process** 116

>The proven system to duplicate your best clients.

Chapter 7 **Your Marching Orders**... 128
Applying what you have learned with a step- by- step action plan.

Forward

What do you do for a living?

It is fitting that this back-to-basics book, one that can help you make more money no matter how well you are doing now, begins at the beginning. As you will see, it starts by trying to get you to answer the most basic question of all: What do you do that allows you to put food on the table.

You have to know what you do for a living and be able to describe it in the proverbial 25 words or less.

If you answered, "I sell stocks and bonds" or "I'm an investment advisor'," or even "I help my clients plan for the future," then you may not be communicating what you really do for a living.

What you really do is sell yourself, every day, in every interaction, with a client or a prospect.

You start at a major disadvantage if you don't know that.

Fortunately for you, Mark Magnacca understands that. Even better, he has explained here—in this short, clearly focused book—how you can maximize your effectiveness by building off your strengths. (He even shows you how you can offset your weaknesses.)

The messages here are simple, but not simple-minded. More important, there is no theory. No preaching from on high. No "words of wisdom" from someone who has never done it. Mark has done what you do for a living, and he has done it well.

Now that he has moved on to coaching financial professionals such as you, he is sharing everything he has learned—the good and the bad—in a straightforward, step-by-step fashion.

What worked for him, and for the advisors he has coached, can work for you. And it *will* work for you, if you put in the effort to truly understand that the product is you, and take the time to learn how you can present that product in the best light.

I wish you well.

Paul B. Brown
Co-author of Customers for Life
Cape Cod Bay, 2003

Introduction

Why Not You?

*You've heard all the buzzwords. The threat of commoditization, globalization, and a lack of differentiation between you and your competition. What these words really mean is that clients have more choices available now than ever before. They need a compelling reason to choose **someone** to advise them. **Why not** give them a compelling reason to choose **you**?*

You're not sure what needs to change. What you do know is that you are working harder, but you're still not satisfied with the results.

*So what can you do? The only thing that is left to do. **Figure out how you can use your biggest resource—you—more effectively**. This book will show you how to do just that.*

Where this all began

I've spent the past decade studying what sets top performers apart. From 1991 to 1998, I built my own independent financial advisory business in the Boston area, called Wellesley Financial Services, Inc. I grew my business primarily through presenting financial education seminars to corporations, associations, and non-profit institutions. As I was building my business, I made almost every marketing mistake possible. In the beginning, I gave seminars where no one showed up. I ran ads that generated no calls. I asked for referrals and received only polite smiles.

I began my career in the independent broker-dealer channel, where there was limited training support. In the absence of a formal training program, I developed my own curriculum, which was, in effect, a trial by fire. As a result, I learned to use every resource I could find. I read dozens of books on a wide range of business topics from sales and marketing to the science of communication. I attended seminars, listened to tapes and found mentors who helped teach me how the game of the financial advisory business is played. After five years of trial and error, I realized something incredible. I had figured out a sales and marketing process that worked and was flexible enough to adapt to changing market conditions. Best of all, it gave me tremendous confidence to keep trying to get better. With each new marketing idea I tried, I learned a new lesson. Sometimes it was subtle and other times it was profound. Either way, the process kept improving, day in and day out. During this time, I not only developed product knowledge, but more importantly, I learned the secrets of building a successful practice.

As I continued my study of what set top performers apart, my investigation took me not only within the financial services industry but also further afield. I studied top performers in a wide range of areas, including Olympic athletes, entrepreneurs and entertainers. Why did I look outside financial services? Because I had an intuitive sense that there was a better way to grow a financial services practice than by following the traditional path that average performers take. And I thought then—and I am convinced now—that stellar performers, no matter what their field, have a lot in common. Among the common denominators:

- They have specific goals.
- They develop a plan to achieve their goals.
- They stick to their plan and can modify it while remaining focused on the objective.
- They have an open mind.
- They are adaptable.
- They don't take rejection personally.
- They push themselves even when they don't feel like it.
- They understand their strengths and their weaknesses.
- They understand the power of working as a team.
- They are coachable.

Let me admit that I had a selfish reason for beginning my study. I was frustrated by the fact that I knew how valuable I could be in helping my existing clients achieve their dreams—and yet I was rarely utilized to my full potential, because my clients didn't understand the full extent of my capabilities.

I knew I could:

- Help them think through the big decisions they needed to make.
- Reduce the emotional component that is so much a part of any financial decision by using a process that I had developed.
- Access my network of people who could help solve almost any financial challenge.
- Educate my clients so they understood why they needed to diversify their portfolios.
- Motivate them to take care of important issues such as estate planning, rolling over their 401k's, and deciding on pension options, to name a few.
- Ask the questions that needed to be asked that most clients never thought about.

And yet, they weren't using me to my fullest.

The light bulb goes on

I finally realized that The Product was "me" when a client of mine told me the "real" reason he worked with me. It was *not* because of the product set or platform that I offered. It was because he trusted me, valued my financial expertise and knew I was looking out for his best interest.

"If I die before my wife," he said, "I want to know that someone I trust and believe in is looking out for her best interests and will be there to advise her about what to do. You know what's important to me and I know you will do what's right for her."

I was amazed. What he was saying was that having me as his advisor gave him peace of mind because he trusted me.

This was the beginning of my new understanding of the true value I brought to my clients. However, I was still frustrated, because I did not communicate this value with clarity to my existing clients or my prospects. This frustration caused me to continue to search for answers to some of the many questions I had:

1. Why was I comfortable dealing with someone with $500,000 to $1 million to invest but not someone with $5 million to $10 million to invest? (You will learn the answer in Chapter 1: **The Mental Thermostat.**)
2. What business was I really in? (You will learn the answer—which I am almost certain will apply to you as well—in Chapter 2: **The Product is You.)**
3. Why could certain people articulate what they did in a succinct and memorable way, and I couldn't? (You will learn how to explain what you do in 30 seconds or less in Chapter 3: **The Elevator Speech.**)
4. How could I find more clients who valued what I could do for them and grow my business. (You will learn the answer in Chapter 4: **Fishing Where the Fish Are.**)
5. How could I credentialize myself and position my value with prospects and clients? (You will learn the answer in Chapter 5: **The Personal IPO.**)
6. How and when do I ask for referrals? (You will learn the answer in Chapter 6: **The Referral Process.)**
7. How could I begin to apply the ideas I had learned? (You will learn the answers in Chapter 7: **Your Marching Orders**)

What I discovered as a result of answering these questions was that success leaves clues. I realized there was a **system and a process** that top advisors use to produce consistent results that meet and exceed their clients' expectations. Most significantly, I recognized that the biggest obstacle preventing me from achieving my goals was not external, it was internal. It was my own beliefs and mindset that were my limitations, not my competition.

As my mindset began to change and I began to implement the system and process I discovered, I was able to accelerate the results I produced for my clients and in my own business.

So you might be wondering, if my system was working so well, why did I sell my practice in 1998? The answer is simple. I found myself looking forward to presenting seminars, because I enjoyed creating compelling seminar content that made people not only think, but act. I liked seeing **"the light bulb go on"** in the eyes of my audience at the moment they said to themselves, "Aha!"

Meanwhile, I was growing increasingly less interested in the day to day financial planning part of the business. In 1997, I reached a crossroads in my career. I had qualified to attend one of my broker-dealer's "top performer" conferences, and I was invited to be a presenter to my colleagues at this conference. At the end of my presentation, I had a conversation with Joe, the president of the firm, about my career dilemma. Joe said, "Mark, you built a great business and you've got a bright future as a financial advisor. For selfish reasons, I would love to have you with us for many years to come. However, I am a believer that people need to do what they love, and it's apparent to me that you love creating and presenting seminars." As I listened to what Joe said, I realized what I really wanted to do and I made a decision to sell my financial business so that I could follow my passion.

Shortly thereafter, I started building my new training and consulting company, called Insight Development Group, Inc. The word *insight* means "an intuitive understanding about the nature of things." My goal was to help my clients develop insight into the best way to market and run their practices.

As I started coaching individual advisors and wholesalers, I began to notice blind spots regarding their marketing efforts and effective strategies to fix them. Word began to spread about the extraordinary results I was achieving by helping my clients penetrate new markets and generate new business. In addition to working with individual advisors and wholesalers, I also worked with insurance and mutual fund companies to help their sales teams develop and implement new marketing strategies.

Throughout this book, I have used the word "advisor" as a generic term to describe people whose titles include financial advisor, financial consultant, investment advisor, investment consultant, insurance agent, CPA, estate planning attorney, and financial planner to name a few. The word advisor is intended to encompass all those financial professionals who are in the business of providing advice and consultation to their clients.

When you are C.A.L.M, you are clear

As I continued to hone and distill my process by working with my clients, I realized there were four things they consistently needed to do to achieve the same breakthrough I had achieved. I call this the C.A.L.M. Process, and it helps my clients:

Create a compelling message
Articulate that message effectively
Locate their target market clients
Motivate those clients to take action

In my experience, the frustration most financial service professionals feel is the result of not knowing how to effectively articulate their value proposition, how to find their target market clients, and how to systematize the process of running their business. They need to think about their business like entrepreneurs, whether they work for a wirehouse or own an independent practice.

What's ahead

Here is how this book is laid out. The next chapter will focus on the "big picture"—strategic objectives and developing a winners mindset. Chapter 2 through Chapter 6 will all be tactically focused around specific tools and ideas you can immediately apply to help grow your business. In the final chapter, I will tie everything together and give you your marching orders so you can begin the process of marketing YOU.

Odds are you're not big on theory. That's good, because I'm not either. If you are interested in how this book can help you, read on.

Chapter 1

The Mental Thermostat:

How to expand your comfort zone
and reset your mental thermostat

What's ahead in this chapter:

Our society has been conditioned to believe there's a magic bullet for every problem. What I've found by studying top performers is that there is no shortcut to success! However, there is a system that when followed can generate measurable results.

This chapter describes the first part of a system designed to help you break the mental barriers that have held you back in the past. Breaking these barriers will free you to transform your business—and ultimately your life.

The glass wall

One day a crack developed in the glass wall that partitioned the aquarium downtown. On one side of the glass wall lived several species of predatory sharks and on the other lived many types of fish, from squid, and tuna, to some unusual tropical species. But no matter how different they looked, all those fish had one thing in common: They would be defenseless in a shark attack.

When the crack was discovered, no one was sure what to do. The senior marine biologist, who had been at the aquarium for many years, said he had seen this happen before in other places where he had worked, and he had the solution.

He recommended that the fish and the sharks be moved to separate holding tanks where the water temperature was kept at the exact temperature as the main tank to make sure all the fish survived.

Once the fish had been removed from the damaged aquarium, he said, all the water should be drained from the tank and the cracked glass replaced with a new piece. Once the repairs were made, the sharks could be returned to one side of the new glass wall and the fish could be safely returned to the other. Yes, the procedure would be expensive, he said, but it would work.

Everyone quickly nodded their heads in agreement, except for one young marine biologist.

"I believe you can replace the glass wall without removing the sharks or the other fish," he said.

The young biologist was immediately met with looks of derision and ridicule. One member of the group said, "Do you know that a shark can smell a single drop of blood up to a mile away and detect the vibrations of another fish up to half a mile away? If you remove that glass partition, there will be a bloodbath."

The young marine biologist respectfully disagreed and convinced the others to agree to replace the glass partition without removing the sharks or the fish.

The rest of the group held their collective breath as a mini crane was brought in. Suction cups were attached to the cracked wall, and the crane slowly raised the cracked piece of glass out of the tank.

As the wall ascended, the sharks turned towards the glass wall with fins down in attack mode. Several of those present cringed as the sharks approached the center of the tank.

But at the very last moment, the sharks turned away.

Why did the sharks, utterly fearless creatures, fail to attack? Because they had been conditioned to believe that they couldn't go past the middle of the tank without slamming into the wall.

It takes the average shark just three times of crashing nose first into the glass to condition its nervous system to know its limitations. And once conditioned, it doesn't try again.

We have a lot in common with sharks

Most human beings act just like the shark when it comes to glass walls—real or imagined.

There are many glass walls that you may have bumped into in the past that no longer exist in reality but still exist in your own mind, thanks to conditioning. How many times have you hit your nose against a glass wall and then come to believe this was your limit?

Think about the glass walls that exist for some people. How often have you heard someone say:

- I don't have enough money
- I don't have the credentials
- I don't have the right education
- I don't have the right family connections
- I could never work with a $50 million account
- I would feel uncomfortable calling a major CEO directly

How many people have gotten their business to a certain level and then become stuck because of a glass wall that prevented forward progress?

The first glass wall I remember being introduced to was when I was about to graduate from high school. Prior to that, like most young people, I truly believed I could do anything I set my mind to do.

On this day, I went to see my high school guidance counselor to tell him I wanted to attend Babson College, in suburban Boston, to study finance and investments. He told me he thought it was an unrealistic expectation for me, based on my SAT scores. The guidance counselor told me that if I had more extracurricular activities or slightly higher SAT scores, then maybe I would have a chance, but as it was I would be better off looking at less competitive schools.

I then read up on Babson College, and the requirements for admittance, and I discovered it would—in fact—be a long shot for me.

In discussing this with my mother, she recommended that I set up an appointment to meet with someone in Babson's admissions department in person. I arrived at the campus early and decided I should take a walk around. As I walked from one building to the next, I knew this was the right place for me, despite what my guidance counselor had said.

I walked back to the admissions office to begin the interview. As I sat down, my interviewer said, "At Babson, we believe the entrepreneurial spirit is more important than just grades and test scores. Why don't you tell me a little bit about what you've done while in high school."

I explained that in addition to going to high school, I bought and restored classic Ford Mustangs, traded in the stock market, and ran a painting business.

The interviewer smiled and said, "No wonder you haven't had much time to study."

By the end of the interview, I knew it had gone well. Several weeks later, I received my early-decision acceptance letter.

As that glass wall shattered, I remember bringing the letter to show my guidance counselor. His reaction: "Oh, they must have changed their admissions policy." Then, apparently feeling defensive, he added, "I just didn't want you to have unrealistic expectations." I know now that this limitation was a reflection of his glass wall based on his past experience.

I recognize that to succeed in life you must continually break through glass walls—both real and imagined.

Breaking down the walls

The most successful advisors I have studied have all developed methods that allows them to get around, over or through the walls they encounter. They have figured out a way to feel at ease in the high-net-worth marketplace. They are not intimidated by how much money somebody has, because they are clear on the value they bring to their clients regardless of whether they have $1 million or $50 million to invest.

The reason I began this chapter by talking about glass walls, is because I have found that breaking through these self-imposed limits is the single most important thing you can do to bring your business to a whole new level of achievement.

Although it is very important to learn new strategies and tactics to grow your business, it is even more important to expand your belief about what is possible and then apply the information you have learned.

To give you an example, I have an acquaintance who purchased a 26-foot sailboat. He and his wife spent months outfitting the vessel with the latest equipment and technology as well as new sails, a lifeboat, and a new sailing wardrobe suitable for the yacht club. However, they never felt confident enough to sail the boat because they never took sailing lessons. So they never left the harbor.

I asked them when they were going to start sailing, and they replied they didn't feel comfortable in the 26-foot boat. So they were going to buy a 30-footer, in which they felt they would be safer.

It never occurred to them that in order to use everything they had purchased, they needed to develop the belief that they could sail. The only way to truly develop that belief was to take sailing lessons from a qualified instructor and then practice what you learned.

I'm sure you can think of many other examples of people who focus on buying all the right stuff but don't know what to do with it! In the financial services business it is not uncommon to find professionals spending thousands of dollars on time-management software, the latest marketing program, or a list of hot prospects. But I have found that in most cases these tools are a poor investment and will remain unused until you make the investment in yourself.

This book is designed to insure that you have developed the right belief system and made the investment in yourself before you launch into specific tactics for growing your business.

The biggest difference between my private coaching clients who have applied what I have taught and those who have not has been the change in their beliefs about their capabilities.

As you proceed in this book, I am going to ask you to push yourself and to stretch your comfort zone. If after reading something, you find yourself saying things like, "I can't do that in my business," or "That won't work here," recognize these thoughts for what they are—self-imposed glass walls.

Let me switch metaphors for a moment. Glass walls function like a **mental thermostat** that constantly keeps us within our Comfort Zone, just as the aquarium's thermostat is set to keep the water at a certain temperature to keep the fish in their comfort zone. But there is a dramatic difference between human beings and fish. *Not only can human beings survive outside their comfort zone, but many people actually thrive.*

Think about the some of the greatest moments of achievement in the past hundred years:

- Neil Armstrong stepping on the surface of the moon.
- President Reagan saying "Mr. Gorbachev, Tear down this wall," as he stood before the Berlin Wall.
- Mark McGwire hitting 70 home runs in 1998.
- Tiger Woods winning the 1997 Masters golf tournament at age 21.
- Thomas Edison trying 10,000 different filaments for his electric light bulb before finding the right one.

All of these peak performers had to reset their mental thermostats and expand their comfort zones. By their actions, they also changed the perception of what was possible. Your willingness to push *yourself* will have a direct impact on the results you achieve from the ideas and strategies covered in this book.

Jonathan, a newly hired advisor at a major wirehouse firm, was facing a comfort-zone dilemma. Although he had excellent credentials, including the fact that he was a lawyer, he was very concerned about a big presentation he had to make the following day to a group of twelve doctors.

His glass wall? He felt inadequate to make this presentation because he lacked experience. (He had been a financial advisor for only a few months.)

In coaching him in preparation for the meeting, I asked Jonathan to tell me how he wanted the doctors to feel at the end of his presentation.

"I want them to feel confident in me," he said.

We determined that in order for this presentation to succeed, he needed a powerful story to communicate the kind of work he had done in the past. As a result of this discussion, he recognized that the investment idea he planned to present was constrained by a number of legal regulations. As soon as he realized that he had a unique ability to explain both the legal aspects and financial details of the investments they were contemplating, he was infused with a new sense of confidence. With this change in mindset there was an immediate change in his physiology and the look on his face. Now he was ready to meet the doctors.

Resetting your Mental Thermostat

Several years ago, during a big winter storm in Boston, we lost our electric power. We were without light, heat, and water for several days. We called the electric company, who told us to be patient and they would do the best they could to get us reconnected. Finally, at 8 o'clock in the evening of the third day, the lights suddenly came back on. It was great to be able to see without candles and flashlights. But the heat had still not come back on.

I called our oil company to explain that our heat wasn't working. The repairman arrived about an hour later with a large toolbox. It was so cold in the house you could see your breath.

He told me that he had a lengthy diagnostic procedure that would help identify the problem. Just before he began to run his tests, he looked at me and said, "Of course, I'm sure you've already tried to press the reset button before you called us."

Suddenly I felt a flush of panic. "What reset button?" I said. He pointed to a large red button located in the center of the box to the left of the furnace, right in front of me.

"Oh, *that* reset button," I said. "No, I haven't pushed it."

With a pained expression he said, "Okay, let's try pushing it."

I reached forward, boldly pressed the button, and the furnace roared back to life. As the repairman was on his way out, I asked him why the reset button was able to get the furnace going again.

He explained that the thermostat had gotten stuck thanks to the cold temperature. The reset button functioned as a way to get the furnace unstuck. Pressing the button, he said, was just like rebooting your computer when it crashes.

Much of what you will learn in this book is like the reset button on that thermostat. It may seem obvious after it is pointed out to you, but when you are standing there in the cold, it is very easy to have a blind spot and not notice that the solution to your problem may be right in front of you.

The one-degree difference

Sometimes only a slight difference in thinking is required to reset your mental thermostat to improve your results. Think about the person who gathers some wood, builds a campfire and hangs his pot over the fire. The fire is burning, the water is almost bubbling, it's at 211 degrees, but it's not boiling. What is required is just a little more, a little extra—in this case just one more piece of wood—and everything changes.

Think what happens when you go from 211 degrees to 212. Now you have steam, and with steam you can move a locomotive, turn a turbine and create electricity. A whole new world opens up at 212 degrees that is unavailable at 211.

Think of how many people came before you and got to 210 degrees, or maybe 211, and never knew how close they were.

Or maybe they stopped because they were afraid. Fear of the unknown, fear of change, fear of failure. Sometimes people lack a support system to help them recover when they meet with the inevitable setbacks.

Lag time

One of the most common reasons people give up too soon, when it comes to marketing and business building efforts, is the concept called "lag time."

Lag time is the gap between beginning something and noticing the result. When you start a fire in a wood stove, for the first five minutes the metal is still cool and it seems as if nothing is happening. Many people give up at this point, because they are unwilling to wait. If you can stay with what you began, soon you will feel the heat, and then it's much easier to keep your fire burning.

It is not much different in business. When I first began to market my financial advisory business through seminars, the results I attained were disappointing. To attract participants to my first seminar, I ran an ad in the local newspaper—once. I remember seeing the ad in the paper and thinking the phone would begin to ring any second and on the other end the people would be clamoring to come to my seminar. I didn't get a single call from that ad—not even a wrong number. I remember arriving at that seminar hoping that it would fill up with people who had decided to come at the last minute. Nobody came. It was just me and my donuts. I decided to do a full rehearsal as if the crowd was present to avoid making the experience a total loss.

Over the coming weeks I tried different strategies, and as I did, I realized the concept of lag time applied to advertising as well. One ad just wouldn't do it.

As I continued my research, I discovered in order for advertising to be effective, people needed to see an ad a minimum of six times, with the best results after ten or more times. Less than six months after my first seminar, I conducted my 10th. This time there were 40 people in a room designed for 30. It was literally a "standing room only" crowd. Half of the attendees came from my advertising effort and the other half came through word of mouth and other centers of influence.

The moral? I didn't feel like doing another seminar after my first failure, but I did it anyway. In my case the lag time was six months before my new thinking and strategies paid a dividend.

Far too many advisors jump from one marketing idea to the next rather than sticking with one long enough for it to make a difference. As a result, they may be missing out on a whole new world of possibility to transform their thoughts into reality

The marathon mindset

Let me give you a personal example of how your attitude can affect your outcome. As far back as high school, I didn't like to run. I never really saw the point and I used to get severe cramps in my legs after running just one or two miles.

I remember watching the news one year as they showed a runner on his hands and knees crawling the last hundred yards to the finish line of the Boston Marathon. He was wrapped in an aluminum blanket, soaking wet from head to toe, with an expression full of pain on his face. I remember thinking how embarrassed he must have been feeling as other runners stepped over him as they ran confidently to the finish line. I remember thinking, "I wonder if I would end up like that guy if I ever ran a marathon."

I admired the ability of marathoners, and marveled at their ability to run more than 26 miles, but the memory of my legs cramping up and the image of the guy crawling to the finish line wrapped in the aluminum blanket kept me firmly in the spectator camp.

In July 2002, my friend Tom came to visit me from California. He told me that he had run his first marathon in San Diego three months earlier and had finished the race with almost no training. I was amazed because he told me he had never run more than a few miles prior to the race.

All of a sudden a seed was planted in my mind that perhaps I could do this too. Tom had stoked my competitive fire, but more importantly, he had changed my belief about what was possible for me. I realized that he was in no better shape than I was, and that if he could do it, I could too. Right then, I made the decision that I was going to run a marathon and finish it.

Using the same systematic approach I used for building my business, I created a plan to accomplish the goal of running a marathon. The first step was to find someone who had run a marathon successfully, to be my coach. I remembered that a friend of mine, Neil Wood, held the marathon record in New Hampshire (with a time of two hours and seventeen minutes), so I asked him to help me achieve my goal. His first suggestion was to read **Marathon,** by Jeff Galloway. I bought the book and realized that the strategy he recommended for people like me, people who had never run more than five miles, was nothing short of revolutionary in its simplicity.

Galloway's recommendation: Run for six minutes and walk for one minute throughout the training period of six months. During this time, increase the mileage by one mile each week, until you reach 26 miles. The strategy for the race itself was also to run for six minutes and walk for one minute throughout the race. This approach allowed new runners to pace themselves and conserve their energy in order to complete the marathon. I couldn't believe that something so simple could really allow me to achieve a goal that I had previously considered unobtainable.

My friend Tom challenged me to run the New York Marathon on November 3, 2002. I had only three months to train for the event, even though I had never run more than five miles in my life.

I followed the simple strategy I had learned from the book, and in October, one month before the race, I ran ten miles—walking one minute for every six I ran—and was amazed at the glass wall I had broken through. I must admit that I didn't actually plan to run ten miles on this day. In fact, I had only planned to run five.

I decided to begin my run while visiting Tom in San Diego. I started running with his brother-in-law, TJ, who was also planning to participate in the New York Marathon.

TJ, who had been training for six months for the New York Marathon, was in great shape. I agreed that I would run the first two or three miles with him and then let him continue on for the rest of his fifteen-mile run. I planned to simply run two and a half miles out and two and a half miles back, for a total of five miles.

We headed out, and when I reached the two and a half mile point, I was feeling pretty good, so I decided to run a little farther with TJ, who was also using the "Galloway method." At about four miles, I decided it was time for me to head back, so we parted company. He told me I could take a shortcut to get home if I didn't want to run back the same way we came.

I started back on the shortcut and got caught up in the new scenery along the way, rather than paying attention to his instructions. About thirty minutes later, I ended up in a neighborhood with a breathtaking view of the Pacific Ocean. I remembered that Tom lived at least five miles from the water, so I knew I had taken a wrong turn somewhere. (I also realized that when you come from New England you are used to the water being to the east, and so your sense of direction can be thrown off when you visit the West Coast. That's my story and I'm sticking to it.)

Anyway, I had a pedometer that measured how far I had run, and I was now at six miles, and still feeling pretty good. I was, however, somewhat concerned about finding my way back, so I decided to stop at a fire station. I explained that I was from out of town and had gotten lost while running. I told them my friend's address, and they rolled their eyes, and said, "You're not even close." They drew me a map and I headed off.

When I reached the eight-mile mark, the scenery began to look familiar. I also realized that my legs seemed to be on "autopilot." I wasn't even consciously moving them and yet I was running as if they had a mind of their own. As I turned the corner, it was getting dark, and I knew that if TJ returned before I did, everyone would be worried about me. It had been almost three hours since I went out for my *five-mile* run. Sure enough, as I approached the house, a group of people were standing in the driveway, and they started cheering as I began my triumphant last sprint to the house.

I looked down at my pedometer, which read 10.3 miles. I couldn't believe I had run so far. My wife and the rest of the group asked me why it had taken me so long to run five miles, and I showed them the pedometer. They were amazed. (Thankfully, TJ had not returned yet, so they hadn't been tipped off to my troubles.)

The day after my big ten-mile run, my legs hurt, but I was actually functioning and I went for a run. The next day, my legs hurt even more, but I persevered. By the third day, my legs were getting better and I began to see the picture in my mind's eye of crossing the finish line in the New York Marathon.

Although the book had recommended that you build up your endurance to 26 miles over a six-month period before the marathon, this was not an option for me because it was now October and the Marathon was in November. I only had one month left to train. The book had also recommended avoiding doing a long run within two weeks of the Marathon, which really gave me just two weeks to get ready.

The night before the big race, I felt a sense of calm, because I had decided that no matter what, I was going to stick to my plan of running for six minutes and walking for one, just as the book instructed. The race began on Sunday morning at 11:00. The starting gun was fired, and we began our trek across the Verrazano Bridge. Six minutes later I was half way across the bridge, and it was time for my walking break. Tom, who had committed to following the plan with me, started walking as well. Moments later, a man dressed in a rhinoceroses costume ran past us. Tom said, "I don't mind walking, but I hate the thought of getting beat by a rhino." As soon as the sixty seconds were up, we started running again. Shortly thereafter, I saw the sign that said mile three and realized I was 10% done.

As we wove through the boroughs of New York City, I was amazed how powerful a force the crowd was in motivating me to keep going. As time wore on, I wondered why everyone seemed to be cheering for Tom and nobody was cheering for me. They knew our names because before the race started we had taped the letters of our names on our sweatshirts. With each mile, people in the crowd would cheer, "Go Tom; Go Mark."

"Here I am at mile six with my name still intact"

But after about ten miles, all I could hear was "Go Tom, go hey," but no one said "Go Mark." I kept wondering who "hey" was. It wasn't until I reached the halfway point and looked down that I realized that the letters M, R, and K had fallen off my sweatshirt, leaving only the letter "A." This explained why I thought people were saying "Go Hey," when in fact they were saying "Go A" (with a New York City accent). I immediately felt a new surge of energy once I realized they were cheering for me too. As I approached mile 20, I realized something else. Many of the people who had passed us earlier in the race were now walking themselves. We were still running for six minutes and walking for one.

At mile 23 I hit my new glass wall. I began to get a serious cramp in my knee and wasn't sure if I could take one more step. Fortunately I could see a medic station up ahead and I decided to stop and ask for help.

"What's the problem," the medic asked.

"I have a sharp pain in my knee.

"Your muscle is probably getting a little stiff because the temperature has dropped and it's pretty cold right now," the medic told me. He then said, "Do you want an aluminum blanket to warm up while you're sitting here?" Remembering the image that kept me from running all these years, I said, "No way."

So the medic applied some sports cream to my knee, and after less than a minute, my leg began to feel better. He said, "You are only three miles away; you're going to make it." With that, I started running again with my friend Tom right by my side.

As we approached the final mile, I felt unusually strong and calm. I thought this must be the "runners' high" that people talk about. I saw my wife cheering for us with 100 yards to go. I knew at this point that I would *not* be crawling across the finish line. As I ran over the finish line, I realized that I felt pretty good and that the strategy I had used had worked. The officials handed me my gold medal for finishing and my wife greeted me enthusiastically. Tom and I had accomplished this goal by working together as a team and sticking to our plan.

My Gold medal team after completing the Marathon- From left to right: Tom, T.J., Mark, Tom, Fred, Pete.

As we toasted our victory with some other runners at a local pub, I realized that something profound had just happened. My old glass wall had shattered, and my mental thermostat had been reset.

For me, this was a powerful example about what all of us can achieve with the right attitude, the right team, a proven strategy, and a willingness to stretch our comfort zones.

Takeaway Lessons

- I've found that one of the most important factors that determines success **is whether or not someone is "coachable."** Are you willing to be coached and reset your mental thermostat? Are you willing to consider new strategies to grow your business?
- **There is a reason why the best performers in all areas of achievement have a coach**. An outstanding coach can help you recognize what makes you unique. A coach can help push you when you feel like giving up and expand what you believe you can achieve. They can also hold you accountable to your commitments.
- Tiger Woods had Butch Harmon; Michael Jordan had Phil Jackson, Bill Walton and Kareem Abdul Jabar (back when he was known as Lou Alcindor) had John Wooden when they played at UCLA. In all these cases, the **coaches helped their players reach a new level of achievement that was previously considered impossible.**
- In my quest to become a marathoner, I not only read **Marathon** by Jeff Galloway, but also was coached by my friend, Neil Wood, a champion marathoner himself.
- **During this journey I will act as your performance coach.** You will need to set aside any preconceived notions you might have about your capabilities and come to the task with an open mind.
- **There are no limits**. You need to remember that many of us have been conditioned to believe in our limitations, sometimes because of our past failures, other times because we don't want to stray from our comfort zone.
- **The definition of insanity is doing the same thing over and over again, and expecting a different result.** Throughout this book, you are going to learn how to do

things differently and open up a whole new world of possibilities.

- **Remember the one-degree difference** and how a little extra effort can reap exponential results.

"Sometimes a moment's insight is worth a lifetime's experience."
Oliver Wendell Holmes

Knowledge Application

Answer these questions to apply what you have learned

1. How else could you have solved the problem of the crack in the fish tank?

2. What are some of the glass walls you have experienced?

3. Can you remember a time in your life when you did something other people said you could never do? What was it?

4. How were you able to accomplish it?

5. Can you remember a time when you pushed yourself to do something even when you didn't feel like it?

6. What made you keep pushing?

Chapter 2

The Product Is You

The best thing you have to sell is you. Here is how to present your
most important product in the best light.

What's ahead in this chapter:

*A client of mine, who used to be a wirehouse broker, had just
started his own independent financial planning practice. During our
first meeting, he said he was worried that he no longer had the trusted
brand name of his previous employer.*

> *"What do you think differentiates you from the
> competition?" I asked. "Is it the products or services
> you offer? Is it the price you charge or the name of the
> broker-dealer with whom you are affiliated?"*
> *"No to all of them," he said.*
> *I then asked him what percentage of his clients
> transferred with him when he left the big firm.*
> *"About 95%."*
> *"Why do you think they came with you?"*
> *"Because they had a relationship with me and not my
> firm."*
> *"Given that," I said, "what is it that you sell,
> ultimately?"*
> *"What I sell is myself."*

*In this chapter you will learn how to create your own personal
brand to distinguish yourself in the marketplace so that people
understand your value. Why is this so important? Because prospective
clients need to be able to sift through the roughly 650,000 people who
call themselves financial advisors to choose you.*

What's your personal brand?

More than 50 years ago, management consultant Peter Drucker started asking his clients a very powerful question: "What business are you in?"

Inevitably, they answered as if he had asked, "What do you do?"

Drucker would always stop and correct them. In the process, he proved that understanding the distinction between what you do and the business you are in is a powerful competitive advantage.

To illustrate this point, think about Starbucks. What business is Starbucks in?

Yes, it sells coffee, but that isn't the reason it gets twice as much for a cup of java as the place down the street.

Starbucks answers the question "What business are you in" by saying it is in the business of *creating an experience*.

In his book *A New Brand World*, Scott Bedbury, the senior vice president of marketing at Starbucks from 1995 to 1998, said executives at the company spent months trying to answer Drucker's misleadingly simple question.

After significant research and an exhaustive debate, they distilled the essence of the Starbucks brand down to: "Rewarding Everyday Experience." They called these three words their **branding touchstone**, designed to insure that every element of the Starbucks brand remain authentic to its purpose.

Just as the touchstone was used in medieval times to test the authenticity of gold, a branding touchstone is used to determine whether something is an authentic part of the brand.

This branding touchstone allowed Starbucks to introduce its "Frappachino" frozen-coffee drink because it was consistent with a *rewarding everyday experience*. It also helped Starbucks avoid getting distracted by certain marketing ideas that were not a fit for their business, such as selling outdoor patio furniture emblazoned with their logo.

In the graph below, which I call the *value chain*, you can see how Starbucks transforms the value of a commodity, a coffee bean, from two cents per cup to $2 per cup by providing a "rewarding everyday experience."

Location		"Role"	Price
At the vine		Commodity	$.01 to $.02
In the can		Product	$.04 to $.05
Take out		Product/Service	$.75 to $1.00
Starbucks		Branded experience	$2.00-$3.00

Why Starbucks is twice as much!

INSIGHT DEVELOPMENT GROUP, INC.

As our economy continues to move toward globalization and as products and services increasingly become commodities, it is more important now than at any time in the past 100 years to make sure you can distinguish what you *do* from the underlying commodity. This is important if you want to be able to charge a premium for your service.

The Commoditization Trap

If the perception exists that what you are offering is the same as everyone else, then you will be paid the least common denominator for that product or service.

"Ten years ago, most financial advisors got paid everything for the transaction and nothing for advice. Today we get paid everything for advice and almost nothing for the transaction," says Doug Dubiel, vice president and senior financial advisor at Merrill Lynch Wealth Management. Just think about how many industries have been commoditized to the point where the only thing on which they can compete is price. Who would have believed that when the securities business was first deregulated in 1975, commissions would drop so low that a traditional stockbroker could no longer compete with the new breed of discount brokers based on price.

The financial services industry has undergone the same commoditization process that has occurred in most other major industries, including computers and automobiles.

By the early 1980s, the Japanese car manufacturers knew they were having trouble competing in the high-priced luxury marketplace. They realized they needed to create a whole new brand to attract a new group of luxury car buyers who generally associated Japanese brand names with low-priced vehicles. So Toyota created the Lexus brand, Honda created Acura, and Nissan created Infiniti to appeal to upscale buyers who were considering other luxury cars like Mercedes Benz, BMW and Cadillac.

This move showed that the Japanese recognized that what was important to buyers in the premium market was different than what was important to buyers in their core markets. Lexus has become one of the most highly rated luxury car companies which most people do not associate with their parent company, Toyota.

How a major industry disappeared in record time

To give you an example of an entire industry that forgot what business it was really in, consider the vinyl record industry. This industry, originally created by Thomas Edison in 1877, had survived many pronouncements of its obsolescence. Although its format has changed from a cylinder to a flat disc, from hard wax to shellac to vinyl, from fast speeds to slow, the phonographic record was essentially unchanged for more than 100 years. During this time, however, the sound quality had improved dramatically. To give you a perspective, in 1983, 209.6 million vinyl LPs were sold. In 1993 1.2 million units were sold. This represents a 99.5 % drop in vinyl record sales in just ten years—one of the fastest implosions of a dominant technology ever seen in the history of American business. How could this have happened so quickly?

I think the best way to communicate the mindset of certain executives in the vinyl record business is to share a quote I often read in my seminars from the back of a Johnny Mathis album from the mid-1960s: "This Columbia guaranteed high-fidelity recording is scientifically designed to play with the highest quality of reproduction on the phonograph of your choice, new or old. If you are the owner of a new stereophonic system, this record will play with even more brilliant true-to-life fidelity. In short, you can purchase this record with no fear of its becoming obsolete in the future."

Think about the significance of that quote in terms of what happened to the vinyl record industry. When compact discs were first introduced in 1982, there were many people who believed, regardless of the many advantages that compact discs offered to consumers, that most people would not switch or replace their cherished vinyl records with compact discs.

However, people did switch by the thousands, because CDs sounded so much better, they didn't scratch or warp, and they were very portable. Not only did customers purchase their new music on compact discs, they also replaced many of their favorite vinyl albums with CDs.

This begs the question: What business were the vinyl record producers really in? They thought they were in the business of producing vinyl records, but in fact they were in the *music distribution* business.

Ironically, compact discs became even more profitable as a distribution vehicle than vinyl records had ever been.

This evolution is ongoing. The next step is distribution of music over the Internet and MP3 players that don't require a compact disc.

Not knowing what business you're *really* in can be perilous to your long-term viability.

When thinking about what business you're really in, try thinking about it from a new perspective. If you sell power tools, ask yourself why people buy an electric drill. *Not for the drill itself, but for the hole it will create.* When people reach for their wallets, what they really want is the result the product or service promises to bring.

What business are YOU really in?

When I ask advisors what business they are in, I often hear the following answers:

- "I'm in the investment business."
- "I sell mutual funds."
- "I sell life insurance."
- "I manage money for wealthy families."

While such answers may be accurate descriptions of what they *do*, they don't describe the business they are *in*.

One way to discover what business you are in is by asking clients why they work with you. Ask them to tell you *what the value you actually provide to them is.*

If you ask them, what you will probably hear is that you sell trust, competence, and peace of mind, not products or services.

The upshot is clear. You are not in the business of selling stocks, bonds, mutual funds or separate accounts. What you really sell is *YOU,* because *the Product is You!* What differentiates you from the competition is you, and the experience you provide your clients.

Regardless of whether you are a part of a major wirehouse firm or a regional independent broker-dealer, virtually all advisors now have access to the same products and services. Therefore, what differentiates you from everyone else is your own personal brand and what your brand means to your target audience.

When most people talk about the business they are really in, they think of it as a *commodity*. They say, "I'm in the computer business; I'm in the insurance business; I'm in the oil business, I'm in the investment business." None of these replies demonstrates any unique value, and in fact such replies often *cheapen* the perception of what you do. Simply changing how you describe what you do can have an impact on how others perceive your value.

Creating your own personal brand

Once you are clear on what business you are really in, then you are ready to think about how to differentiate yourself in the market. I call this process creating your own personal brand.

When people think of the word branding, most think about some of the greatest brands in our society, such as McDonalds, Coca-Cola, Mercedes-Benz and Nike. But it is more than possible for all of us to create our own brands.

To fully realize how you can benefit from what large companies have learned about creating and managing their brands, let me give you some background on where the modern definition of branding actually came from.

Most people think that the reason cattle were branded was simply for identification purposes. While this is true, it is not the whole story. At the turn of the century, cattle were shipped to the stockyards of Chicago from all over the U.S. Buyers in the stockyards needed to be able to decide quickly which cattle they wanted to purchase. It didn't take them long to realize that certain cattle ranchers cared for and nourished their cattle properly, while others simply fattened them up and were happy to sell a diseased or otherwise unhealthy animal. Thus, the physical brand on the cow became a sure way to decide whom you wanted to do business with and whether you were willing to pay a premium. Each ranch's brand became a shorthand tool to help buyers make purchasing decisions quickly, based on the reputation of the ranch.

The most powerful way to clearly establish your brand value is by understanding what makes your product unique. Consider a symbol you see on the road every day. When you see a three-pointed star inside a circle on a car, what immediately comes to mind?

When Daimler-Benz AG decided in 1909 that it needed a distinctive trademark, Gottlieb Daimler's sons remembered that their father had once drawn a star to mark the location of their home on a photograph, saying that one day such a star would shine in approval above his factory.

Today, the simple, elegant star inside the circle instantly says "Mercedes-Benz" throughout the world.

What do you have? Why should people care?

Until you understand what makes you unique, it is very difficult to really know who in the marketplace will most highly value what you do.

Do you know who Ralph Lifshitz is? I'll bet you do, although he is better known by his brand name, Ralph Lauren. Do you think that the name Lifshitz would ever have become synonymous with elegance, style, and fashion?

Ralph Lifshitz is a perfectly good name, but probably not one that would have easily become associated with the world of Chanel, Bill Blass, and Armani.

Ralph Lifshitz, who was born in the Bronx, changed his name while working as a fledgling fashion designer in the mid-1950s. In 1968, he founded Polo for Men. His clothing brilliantly evoked old money and country-house life for upwardly mobile America. He became well-known for his unique advertising, which promoted the Ralph Lauren image and brand. It is highly unlikely that millions of men all over the world would proudly sport a logo by Lifshitz, but simply by changing the name to Ralph Lauren, he was able to change the perception of value.

By using your branding matrix, you can determine the essence of what you want to communicate and make sure what you present remains authentic to that essence. If you work for one of the major wirehouse firms, you can co-brand by taking advantage of your firm's brand identity and your personal brand identity. Several of my coaching clients who are working within a team have built their own identities within their firm by deciding on a name for their group and marketing it accordingly. Independent advisors can either use their own name or create a corporate identity, depending upon their branding touchstone.

As you will see in the upcoming chapters, understanding what you want to communicate about your brand is only part of the overall puzzle we are putting together. But it is a critical part.

Brand Blunder

One of the most profound blunders in the history of branding was committed by a company with one of the strongest brands in the world: Coca-Cola. When you think about the real value behind Coke, you realize it is not really the secret formula, which any decent chemical laboratory could certainly crack. The real value of the company is its brand equity and the distribution network for what is essentially carbonated, flavored, sugar water.

Several years ago, Pepsi Cola created what was called the Pepsi Challenge with the goal of proving that people liked the taste of Pepsi better than Coke. There were a number of televised taste tests where consumers would drink both soft drinks—and then vote on which one they liked better. Consistently, even Coke drinkers seemed to say they preferred the taste of Pepsi.

In his book, *The End of Marketing as We Know It,* Sergio Zyman, Coca-Cola's former chief marketing officer, explains how the company decided to do its own taste tests.

The result was that Coca-Cola discovered Pepsi was not lying. In fact, in blind tests, consumers consistently preferred the taste of Pepsi to Coke. In particular, they thought the taste was much sweeter and smoother, according to Zyman. As a result, Coca-Cola decided to change their formula and introduce New Coke.

When New Coke was introduced in 1985, there was a revolt throughout the U.S., as consumers protested the new product. So Coca-Cola stopped production of New Coke and reintroduced old Coke, which they dubbed "Coke Classic," 77 days later.

How could such a highly respected company make such a big mistake?

What the Coca-Cola Corp. missed was that a huge part of what makes products or services valuable is intangible.

The same is true for your relationships with your clients. A large part of the value clients derive from their advisors is not just a result of investment performance, but rather the many intangible qualities that give clients an overall feeling of security.

It is difficult to measure how people *feel* about a particular product or service. What people *associated* with the taste of Coke was far more valuable than how it *tasted* compared to Pepsi. Coke had spent 100 years building its brand with a consistent message and taste, and only after the results of this blunder did they come to understand the true value their product offered. The Coke brand meant something to millions of people, and changing the taste affected people's perception of and associations with the product, because it was no longer consistent with their past experience.

As you begin to formulate the brand you want to have, remember that **the most important reason to brand in the first place is to differentiate yourself from the competition.** It is the uniqueness rather than the sameness that makes a brand valuable, whether your product is Coke or financial wealth management.

Psychic Real Estate

I call the process of understanding the associations you want to create in the mind of your target clients *creating psychic real estate*. Psychic real estate is the words, pictures and feelings people associate with a product or service.

If I say to you, "Plop, plop, fizz, fizz, oh what a relief it is," most people will immediately think of the old Alka Seltzer commercial. They'll not only remember the commercial, but most people can even see the picture of the two white tablets fizzing in a glass of water in their mind's eye. That image is the psychic real estate that Alka Seltzer owns. They literally own a little piece of real estate in your mind.

- Who owns the psychic real estate for hamburgers?
- Who owns the psychic real estate for copy machines?
- Who owns the psychic real estate for online books?
- Who owns the psychic real estate for "safe" cars?

If you said McDonalds, Xerox, Amazon, and Volvo, you can go to the head of the class.

One of the interesting things about psychic real estate is that, generally, people only associate one or two primary things with a particular company. For example, McDonalds also sells Fillet of Fish and Chicken McNuggets, but most people associate McDonalds with its hamburgers. The same goes for you: People can generally remember only one or two key ideas about who you are and what you do. The biggest mistake people make when creating psychic real estate is trying to have their personal brand be associated with too many things. Amazon.com sells electronics, holds auctions, and sells music—but they are known first and foremost for books. After you create a book-buying relationship with Amazon, you are more likely to do business with it in one of its sub-categories.

For advisors, I have found that those who specialize in two or three key areas are consistently more successful than those who try to cover all the financial bases, from stocks to mutual funds to insurance, estate planning, options, 401k's, etc.

When you consider your brand, remember that if you want to be unique, you can't be all things to all people. There is great power in specializing in those aspects that truly make you unique. It is much easier to commoditize a general practitioner in medicine, law or financial advice than it is to commoditize a specialist. This is not to say that you must specialize to such an extreme that you can't discuss a wide range of issues. Just recognize that it is easier to build your own personal brand around a core idea than it is to build it around many individual parts.

Are you a retirement-planning specialist? An estate-planning specialist? An executive-compensation specialist? It is possible that your brand could connote the fact that you are a generalist who is able to help your clients with almost any financial issue. The downside to this approach is that when your advice is questioned, there will always be someone else who is a specialist in that arena who will be perceived as knowing more than you do.

Don't like your neighborhood? Move.

What if you don't like the psychic real estate you currently own? Change it! Here is an example of a company that did just that.

When you think of Subaru, you probably think of Crocodile Dundee driving around the Outback in, well, a Subaru Outback. Did that help them sell station wagons? Not by itself. Subaru is a great example of a company that repositioned itself using a specific attribute that allowed it to become well-known and to own a specific piece of psychic real estate in the process.

By 1993, Subaru car sales had plunged 60% from their peak seven years earlier. The company was expected to lose $1 billion that year.

Subaru had tried to build its reputation on the tag line "Inexpensive—and built to stay that way." As an advertising slogan, it was fine, but it did not connect with the market on an emotional level. "We were competing with Honda, Toyota, and Nissan and were fighting to be No. 3 on the shopping list," according to George Muller, who took over as president in 1993. The company needed a better way to bond with consumers. Muller began to ask himself, "What are we good at?" He began to think about the psychic real estate Subaru could own. The answer was *all-wheel-drive*. He dropped every front-wheel-drive vehicle from his line-up and made a commitment to sell nothing but all-wheel-drive cars as a way of differentiating Subaru from Toyota, Honda and Nissan.

Muller then went further. He actually transformed the psychic real estate of all-wheel-drive, because he was concerned that many drivers in California and Florida equated all-wheel-drive with driving in snow country. The new message: All-wheel-drive made Subarus grip the road better not just in snow and ice but also in rain and even on dirty pavement.

As a result of its new strategy, Subaru went from selling 104,000 cars in 1993 to 148,000 cars by 1998. Better yet, by repositioning itself and edging up the luxury and price scale, Subaru earned more profit per vehicle than ever before. As Subaru shows, if you don't like the psychic real estate you currently own, change it.

Think about what you want your personal brand to connote in the marketplace. To help you navigate through this process, you can use the following model and template called the Advisor Branding Matrix:

Sample Advisor Branding Matrix

#	Element	Description	Advisor Answers
1	Current Psychic Real Estate	What psychic real estate do I presently own?	
2	Desired Psychic Real Estate	What psychic real estate do I want to own?	
3	What makes me unique?	What unique attributes and abilities of mine are marketable	
4	Marketing Tools	The tools I use to generate new business	
5	External Barriers	Real world roadblocks	
6	Internal Barriers	Self-imposed roadblocks	
7	Branding Touchstone	Three words that help you remain authentic to your purpose	
8	Who is my target market?	Who are those who can and will decide to pay for my service?	
9	Referability	How easy is it for my clients to refer me?	
10	Communication Strategy	How do I presently communicate my value to prospects?	

Note: A truly professional advisor should be absolutely clear about who they are, what they stand for and how they can and should communicate this to the world. This matrix can act as a foundation to speed up the process. (Adapted from Tony Jeary-High Performance Resources Branding Matrix. Used with Permission. www.tonyjeary.com)

Why do you need a personal biography?

After you have completed your branding matrix you will be ready to create your own personal biography.

Why is this necessary? Well, think of it this way. What if there were a way to begin creating the right associations before prospective clients even met you in person?

One of the most powerful tools for advisors for creating psychic real estate in the minds of their prospects and clients is a *personal biography*.

Think about what the average business card tells the prospect about the value you offer your clients. It tells them almost nothing! Beyond that, it serves to commoditize you because it typically contains the same information everyone else at your firm and all your competitors have on their cards as well: Your name, company name, address, phone number, fax number and e-mail address. This information is useful for people when they want to contact you, but it does nothing to communicate why people should call you and not the other 650,000 financial advisors in the U.S.

As a general rule, salespeople do not use biographies because they do not believe it is necessary. However, when people think about making decisions that put their life savings at stake, most investors want to know something about the character and competence of the people with whom they are entrusting their money.

Do you have customers or clients?

There's another reason for having a biography, and it has to do with the difference between customers and clients. Many people use the terms interchangeably, but these two words have very different meanings.

Does an accountant or a lawyer have customers or clients? Clients, of course. Does Wal-Mart or Sears have customers or clients? You are a customer of WalMart or Sears, not a client.

The distinction centers on whether you have a transactional relationship or an advisory relationship. Almost all professional services have clients rather than customers. This is why I recommend that advisors who want to develop an ongoing relationship with clients create a biography that positions themselves as advisors rather than salespeople. This contrasts with most transactional salespeople, for whom background, character, and competence are not as important as the company they work for.

For example when you walk into Wal-Mart and ask the salesperson what aisle the diapers are in, you would be put off if they handed you their biography before sending you to aisle 7.

A financial salesperson who acts primarily as an order taker typically does not need a personal biography. For example, most people calling a sales representative at a major discount brokerage firm on a 1-800 number don't really care about the background and qualifications of the sales representative. This is because they already know what they want to purchase and they're simply giving instructions to the sales representative. In fact, if you call back, you are not going to talk to the same sales representative twice, except by chance. So knowing more about the sales rep's background and credentials is of no value.

But you aren't an order taker. You are an advisor. So you need a biography.

Who else uses a biography? CEOs, doctors, academics, authors, speakers and experts in almost every field. Using one will put you in good company.

What will a biography accomplish for you? It answers most of the questions prospects and clients might have about you that they may not feel comfortable asking you directly. It communicates your character and competence and it helps to discover common ground between you and your prospect.

The biography is designed to answer the two most important questions prospects ask themselves. "Can I trust you?" and "Are you qualified to help me?"

In our culture, most of us have been taught that it is not proper to talk about yourself for fear of seeming self-important or bragging. As a result, in a sales context, people often say very little about themselves or their background.

When you work at one of the major consulting firms, there is a different mindset about the use of a biography. These firms understand that they are really selling the collective intelligence of individual people. As a result, it is very common to use the biographies of different team members when selling their services. In many ways, the statistics that are used for athletes in baseball, football, golf, etc., serve as a quasi biography. This background information connotes ranking and qualification.

Mark Magnacca Bio (Sample 1)

INSIGHT DEVELOPMENT GROUP, INC.
MAKING THE BEST EVEN BETTER

Mark Magnacca
President, Insight Development Group

Mark Magnacca, President of Insight Development Group, is an internationally recognized peak performance strategist and sales coach. Mark's mission is to help his clients boost their performance to a higher level of achievement.

Prior to founding Insight Development Group, Mark co-founded Wellesley Financial Services, a financial education and investment management firm. During that time, he was responsible for creating innovative practice development and business building strategies. These strategies have become the foundation for his Results Accelerator Series Training program for Financial Advisors.

Insight Developments Group's seminar programs have been utilized by many leading corporations including:

- Merrill Lynch
- Smith Barney
- INVESCO
- Fidelity Investments
- TD Waterhouse and
- MetLife

They have also been featured in both print and television media including:

- The New York Times
- USA Today
- The Wall Street Journal
- Registered Rep
- Financial Planning and
- CNN's Moneyline.

Mark is a graduate of Babson College where he majored in finance, investments and communication.

Mark enjoys boating, hiking, windsurfing and reading. He resides in the Boston area with his wife Kristen and son Cole.

Mark Magnacaa
6 Thayer Street
Upton, MA 01568
TEL 888 249-4747
FAX 508 590-5692
mark@insightdevelopment.com
www.insightdevelopment.com

John Jones Advisor Bio (Sample 2)

John Jones
CFP Financial Advisor

Putting your financial needs first is my job. Many of my clients are very serious about managing their money responsibly in order to achieve their financial goals. That's where I come in. Working together, we design a sound, disciplined plan to help meet your financial needs.

SERVICES OFFERED:
Personal financial planning including planning for retirement, asset allocation, investments, education, risk protection, taxes and estate planning.

SPECIALIZED TRAINING:
Comprehensive training in financial planning and products. All licenses and registration required to transact business including National Association of Securities Dealers (NASD) registration and state securities and insurance licenses. Registered as an investment advisor agent of American Express Financial Advisors, Inc. in states where required.

DESIGNATIONS:

- Certified Financial Planner

NOTABLE ACCOMPLISHMENTS;

- American Express Financial Advisors, Inc.
- President's Recognition Award, 1999

PERSONAL INFORMATION;

- Married with two children
- Hobbies include white water rafting, water skiing, hiking
- Graduate of Boston College

There are many applications where you can use your personal biography;

1. Send it to prospects prior to meeting them in person.
2. Include it with your seminar kit at seminars you present.
3. Use it to introduce yourself to orphan accounts that you are taking over.
4. As a tool to help make getting referrals from your existing clients more productive.

You will find 10 questions below that you can answer to help you create your personal biography.

Some of the options to consider for your biography are whether or not you want to use a full 8.5 x 11 one-page version or a 4.25 x 11 half-page version. You also need to decide whether or not you want to include your picture. I believe that including your picture is important in helping prospective clients get to know you even before they meet you in person.

Once this questionnaire is completed, you will need compliance approval and you'll have to decide on the format to use. Regardless of how much information you decide to include, this is a powerful tool that can give you a competitive edge.

Here are some questions that can help you begin your personal biography.

1. How long have you been in the industry and what year did you join your firm?

2. What is your title and primary responsibility?

3. What is your specialty and what markets do you focus on?

4. What is the first thing a client should know about you?

5. Describe a past experience that you have had that is valuable in your present role.

6. What makes you unique and sets you apart?

7. What do you like most about your work and why?

8. What is your educational background?

9. What professional certifications and designations do you hold?

10. Please give us a little personal information about yourself, such as whether you are married and if you have children, hobbies, charitable activities or special interests.

You have just completed the first step in creating your own personal biography.

Do You Have the Right Stuff?

I have had the unique opportunity of working with hundreds of people in helping them create their personal biographies. I have found that many talented people feel inadequate about some part of their credentials. Some feel they don't have enough product knowledge, experience, or educational credentials. Some feel they are too young; some feel they are too old. The best part of doing this exercise is that it forces you to think about the value you actually deliver to your clients.

Top Gun Breaks the Barrier

Top Gun Pilot as he breaks through the sound barrier

At one of the sessions I facilitated for a group of newly hired advisors at a major financial services company, one participant felt uncomfortable about doing the biography exercise because he felt his educational background and industry experience would hinder rather then help him. Still, he was willing to participate in our "Hot Seat" exercise where I interviewed him in real time using the biography questions. I discovered that he had been a Top Gun Navy pilot for nine years and had left the service with an honorable discharge to begin a new career as a financial advisor. As he looked around the class, he felt inadequate, because he thought everyone else had so much more product knowledge and experience than he did. I began to ask him a series of questions, and I listened carefully to his responses.

"What kind of plane did you fly?" I asked.

"An F-14," he said.

"Where did you fly these planes?"

"I patrolled the no-fly zone in Iraq set up after the Gulf War."

"Were you ever shot at?"

"I was fired upon several times as part of an on-going game of cat-and-mouse."

"Was managing risk part of your job as a pilot?"

"Absolutely."

I then asked," How much does an F-14 cost?"

"About $40 million."

"So let me understand this. The U.S. government trusted you enough to allow you to fly a $40 million airplane in which you had to make life-or-death decisions every day. And you are not sure whether this has any relevance to helping your clients make investment decisions?"

"Well . . ."

I then asked the rest of the class what they thought, and as so often happens, other people were able to see aspects of what he was capable of because they were not constrained by his own preconceived notions about his value.

One of the participants said, "As a former military officer myself, I would be more interested in working with you than with someone else, because you can probably understand my background and beliefs better than someone who has never served in the military."

Another one said, "The ability to stay calm and cool under pressure is so important in communicating to clients and giving them an understanding of the long-term context of the market's volatility. You've already faced far greater pressure than the Dow dropping 500 points in a day, and you've handled it successfully."

As we began to peel the layers back, this former-pilot-turned-financial advisor quickly realized that what he had thought was his greatest weakness was in fact his greatest strength. He realized that people bought *him* first—not the products or services, and that the area he should focus on first was working with other retired military officers. All of a sudden, his objections about his lack of experience faded away because he realized all he needed to do was get in front of the right kind of people for him. Using a personal biography would allow him to communicate that he was an officer and build common ground with his prospects before they even met him.

He then realized that just as he was part of a team in the military, he was part of a team now. In the military, each team member had a specific job, and it's the same as a financial advisor. He was now part of a new team in financial services. There were several people in his office, including his manager, who were willing to help him succeed. Once he realized the business he was really in, and the support he had, he said, "I'm ready to begin."

Whether you choose to use a personal biography with your clients or not, the process of creating one inevitably leads to more clarity, more focus, and more confidence, because you recognize the real value you can deliver to your clients.

Takeaway Lessons

- **You are indeed the message.** More than any product you put before your clients, you are selling yourself.
- **What do you stand for?** Are you clear about the value you are offering your clients and prospective clients?
- **Are people clear about that?** Do your clients understand what you are offering? It is one thing for you to be clear about what value you offer, but your clarity doesn't help much if you aren't communicating it to your clients.

"What you do speaks so loud that I cannot hear a word you say."
Ralph Waldo Emerson

Knowledge Application

Answer the following questions to help you determine your value proposition:

1. What business are you really in?

2. What is the commodity you sell?

3. What are people really buying from you?

4. What are the words, feelings, and images they link in their minds when thinking of you?

5. What makes you unique?

6. How do you want to be remembered after you have a meeting with one of your clients?

7. If your best client could remember just one thing about you, what should it be?

8. What do you believe your best clients associate with you right now?

Chapter 3

The Elevator Speech

How to quickly and effectively communicate what you do in 30 seconds or less to make a lasting impression.

What's ahead in this chapter:

Most people feel anxious when they're asked, "What business are you in?" In this chapter you will learn how to answer this question in a compelling and memorable way.

Why is this so important? Because you never get a second chance to make a first impression. The way you answer the question, "What do you do for a living?" usually determines whether or not people even want to listen to you.

You will also learn how to harness the power of using stories and scripting to communicate your message.

The lobby . . . PLEASE!

The following is a story about what happened to me before I crafted my Elevator Speech.

In 1997, I attended a conference sponsored by my broker-dealer at The Breakers Hotel in Palm Beach, Florida. I was wearing a shirt with the name "Commonwealth Financial Services" embroidered on it. I stepped into the elevator on the sixth floor and pressed "L" for the lobby. A man in his mid-50s standing on the other side of the elevator noticed my shirt and said, "I see your shirt says Commonwealth Financial Services. What does Commonwealth Financial do?"

Just then I felt an overwhelming desire to explain what I did. I had all these thoughts in my head, but I wasn't sure which one I should say first. Eventually, I said, "Well, Commonwealth Financial Services is an independent broker-dealer that clears the financial transactions I make for my clients."

I noticed the man's face begin to wrinkle with confusion as he said "Oh."

So I said, "I actually own my own business, called Wellesley Financial Services."

"What does Wellesley Financial Services do?"

I told him that we were in the money management business.

"Oh," he said again. "So, does Commonwealth manage the money for your clients?"

"No," I said, "they simply function as a middleman."

At this point we arrived in the lobby and I'm sure the man was greatly relieved to be getting off the elevator. I realized that I had not only confused him but probably did more damage to my credibility than if I had said, "I could tell you what I do, but then I would have to kill you."

I am sure many of you have had a time in your life when you were unable to articulate what you do quickly and effectively. The fact is, as our economy becomes more specialized, explaining what we do has become more complex. After this exchange in the elevator, I vowed to invest some time in coming up with a clear, intriguing answer to the question "What do you do?"

I already knew that copying what most other people said wouldn't help me much. In talking to other financial professionals, I'd heard them say, "I am a stockbroker," or "I am an insurance agent," and I realized that just the mention of those words dredged up associations in my mind that were both unpleasant and, quite frankly, boring. I needed something better. And that is what sent me on my quest to learn how I could explain what I do for a living in a simple, clear and compelling way.

How to ring the bell

What you are about to learn could "ring the bell" for your business as well as provide you with tremendous peace of mind, rather than the normal agitation and nervousness that accompanies your having to answer the "What do you do?" question in public.

The goal behind this exercise is simple: By the time we are done, you will be able to effectively communicate what you do in a compelling way in thirty seconds or less.

During the IPO frenzy of the late 1990s, this concept of creating an Elevator Speech was raised to an art form by a handful of people seeking funding for their startup companies. I remember attending a venture capital breakfast where the people who had money sat on one side of the room and the entrepreneurs who wanted money sat on the other. Each entrepreneur seeking funding had 60 seconds—a fairly long elevator ride—to explain his or her concept in a way that generated interest.

Most of them were unable to do it. It was difficult to watch people who were so obviously well-educated and intelligent stumble and stammer their way through their allotted 60 seconds. People who had worked so hard on their business plans and financial spreadsheets had unfortunately forgotten that these 60 seconds were what really mattered.

But those who really worked at it were rewarded—handsomely.

One entrepreneur at the breakfast explained what he did in the form of a *story,* and when he finished and sat down there was an immediate buzz in the room as everybody began talking about the merits of his concept.

You may wonder if there is any science behind making a message compelling. The answer is a resounding YES! One of the fundamental concepts that adult learning experts all agree on is that *the best way to teach something new is to build on information people already have.*

The converse is also true. Most adults, defined as anyone over 21, have learned to be skeptical about anything with which they are unfamiliar. So you want to make sure that new information is presented in a way that makes the listener feel comfortable. And there is no better way to do that than by presenting the key points in the form of a story.

The magic of stories and metaphors

Throughout history, stories and metaphors have been a powerful way of informing and communicating ideas to people. As you think about what you have read in this book up to this point, I would bet that most of what you remember are the stories and metaphors I have used to make a point. That isn't surprising. The word metaphor comes from the Greek words *meta,* meaning "beyond," and *pherein,* meaning "to carry." The literal definition is, therefore, "to carry beyond." A metaphor gives the listener the ability to carry an existing understanding of something beyond its original context and into a new one.

The most successful communicators in our culture have all mastered the art of using stories and metaphors to make their point.

When Ronald Reagan said, "It's morning in America again." he captured a powerful idea—"We are starting over again"—which was exactly what most Americans wanted to hear at that time.

Good stories do four things that help improve communication.
1. They cause a listener to relax.
2. They cause a listener to become less critical.
3. They contain vivid images and potent messages.
4. They flow from one thought to another and have the ability to capture the imagination.

The obvious question then is how do you tell a great story? One simple answer: You practice.

The science of storytelling

One of the significant common denominators that have set great communicators apart from most people is their ability to practice and rehearse their stories and message until they can be told with ease.

There is a major unintended consequence of rehearsing your Elevator Speech so that you know it well enough that you could be awakened in the dead of night and still recite it perfectly. That is the ability to be a more effective listener. Unlike many people, who are focused solely on what they are going to say rather than what they are hearing, if you already know what you want to say, you will really be able to listen. (Read more about the importance of listening at the end of the chapter.)

Scripting

Okay, you understand the need to rehearse. But what are you going to rehearse? Your "script," of course.

There is a tremendous power in taking the time to script in advance what you want to say, before you say it. Part of this power results from the ability to pre-determine how other people will react to what you say, and part of this power comes from your ability to determine how you want to present the words you want to say.

When most people watch a movie, they are not conscious of the fact that the actors are really speaking lines from a script. This is because the actors have rehearsed sufficiently so that they have made their lines their own.

The words you choose to describe your product or service help create psychic real estate in the mind of your target audience. In addition, the questions you choose to ask a client or prospect focuses the attention of your listener in a certain direction. Anyone who doesn't have certain questions to ask a prospect, and a variety of prepared responses to their likely questions, is at a disadvantage.

Top performers in almost every field, whether it is sales, consulting, or law, all take the time in advance to prepare the questions they will ask as well as the responses to questions from others. The reason this is so powerful is because the words we use literally affect people's perceptions and the associations they make in their minds. The words you choose help to create psychic real estate either positively or negatively.

Scripts come in many different forms. The one common feature? They work. Let's review a few of them to see just how powerful this concept is.

Musical Scripts

Think about how a certain song playing on the radio can immediately put you into the state of mind you've previously associated with that song. A song can often trigger an association with an event or person from the past. A song is simply a script set to music.

While I am not suggesting that you sing to your clients, I want you to be aware of how the words in songs produce powerful emotional reactions in people and how you can set the tone with what you say and how you say it.

Famous scripts

There are scripts that create associations that have affected our entire culture. None of the quotes below were spontaneous; all of them were carefully thought out and rehearsed before they were said.

"That's one small step for man and one giant leap for mankind." —Neil Armstrong

"Ask not what your country can do for you, but what you can do for your country." —John F. Kennedy

"Four score and seven years ago." —Abraham Lincoln

"I am not a crook." —Richard Nixon

Think about the psychic real estate these comments hold in your mind.

Hollywood Scripts

How many times have you watched the Academy Awards and seen an award winner walk up to the podium and say, "I can't believe it, I don't know what to say."

I saw an awards program that was being broadcast worldwide to an audience estimated at 1 billion people. There were only five finalists in each category. When the winner was announced, he walked up to the microphone and said, "I didn't prepare anything to say because I didn't think I was going to win." Think of how ridiculous that sounds. If you had a 20% chance of winning, wouldn't you prepare something?

At the other end of the spectrum are people who, in the absence of a script, drone on and on. I remember watching one acceptance speech during which the actor started thanking people from her high school, her college, her neighborhood, her studio executives, her family, until the show actually cut to a commercial break to interrupt her. By that point she had used up so much time that the following actors had only had a few moments left for their own speeches.

Compare this with the actor who wins the award, walks up to the microphone, pulls out a small piece of paper and says, "I would like to thank the Academy, my director, my co-stars, and my wife and family for all their support while I was making this movie. Thank you."

Isn't it ironic that actors, who understand the value of a good script more than most people, are prone to making the same exact mistakes as everyone else when they try to *wing it*.

Airline Scripts

Speaking of winging it, think of the script that flight attendants use on a plane when they say, "In the unlikely event of a water landing, your seat cushion functions as a flotation device." Compare that with a script that says, "In the unlikely event of a crash, your seat cushion is also a life preserver." Think of the words, pictures and feelings produced in you by these two statements. The first one generates an image of a plane gently landing on the surface of the water and you floating away while holding on to your seat cushion. The second immediately conjures up fire, screaming, and the mayhem associated with a plane crash. The effect of the words "water landing" versus "crash" is profound.

Financial Advisor Scripts

This concept applies to the words you choose to describe the products and services you offer. I remember once, during my first year in the business, I told a client that I get paid out of the "load" on the mutual fund. My prospect looked at me and said, "You get paid from the *what*?" "The 'load' is the word for the commission charged when you buy this fund," I said. Think of the psychic real estate I was creating with that script!

I soon realized that I needed a better way to communicate this message, because prospects asked the question frequently. I developed several different approaches and metaphors to help communicate the value I brought to my clients and how I was compensated. I remember talking to a client who needed to receive a consistent guaranteed monthly income, who was originally against the idea of an annuity. Nevertheless, I showed him three different immediate annuity quotes and explained the terms and conditions of each.

He immediately tensed up and said, "I thought annuities were a bad investment."

"Why do you think that?"

"Because my grandfather had an annuity that was supposed to pay him his retirement. He died only three months after he retired, and the money was kept by the insurance company."

I said, "I know what you are talking about, and the kind of annuity I am recommending is different. Do you know how when somebody wins the lottery for $1 million, they only get $50,000 a year for twenty years?"

He nodded in agreement.

"That $50,000," I continued, "is actually an annuity payment that is paid to the winner on a yearly basis. The word annuity simply means the payment of a fixed sum of money at regular intervals of time. If a lottery winner dies before the 20 years is up, his beneficiaries receives the balance of the payments. This is the same way the annuity I am recommending for you works."

I saw the tension in his face fade away. "Oh, now I understand," he said. "How do you get paid for this?"

I said, "Do you know how when you buy a ticket from a travel agent, you don't pay them a commission directly, but rather they are paid by the airline?"

"Yes."

"Well, the way I get paid is very similar, because I receive a commission directly from the insurance company that issues the annuity."

He nodded in agreement. "Okay, I understand. Which one do you recommend for me?"

I realized how powerful using stories, scripts and metaphors were in communicating complex ideas in a simple and understandable fashion. Compare this with the standard script of somebody explaining an immediate annuity: "The payment you will receive from an immediate annuity is based upon the distribution term you choose. The annuity factor used to determine this payment is based upon mortality tables created by the insurance industry. You can choose from several annuitization options including life, life plus ten years, etc."

This was the kind of explanation I first used. Not surprisingly, it typically caused confusion and frustration among my clients. Once I began to integrate the use of scripting into my presentations, I found that my clients not only understood the ideas I presented, they could even communicate how it worked to their family and friends.

My annuity story was extremely effective until the travel industry revamped their compensation structure and made the metaphor obsolete. When this happens, you simply find another metaphor. As I transitioned to the advisory model in my own business, I had to explain why this new approach of being paid on "assets under management" made sense for both my clients and myself.

Here's what I said to a new client: "Do you know how one of the frustrations many people had with traditional stockbrokers is they paid a commission to buy and a commission to sell and always wondered whether the stockbroker's motives were in the client's best interest? Well, what I do is take a totally different approach. My clients pay me a 1% management fee on their total account value and there are no commissions paid to buy or sell stocks or mutual funds. What this does is insure that my goal is in alignment with their goal, which is to see the value of their account grow over time."

One of the best ways to begin applying this concept is to start your own *script book* with phrases that you have found to be effective. Now and then, you will find that you have a great answer to an objection, or you will hear someone else with a great answer to an objection. You may also hear a great story that communicates the fundamental idea you want to present. Start writing these scripts down in a notebook. In a relatively short period of time, you can distill this list into a few choice responses to the vast majority of questions and concerns related to your products and services.

Here are a few choice responses to one of the most common objections advisors hear: "I want to think about it."

- "You need to think about it? Good. Let's think about it out loud. You know, sometimes two heads are better than one."
- "Have you ever made a financial decision like this that turned out well? How did you do that?"
- "I'm curious, what exactly do you want to think about?"

Whether these responses work for you or not, recognize that having an effective response to the statement "I want to think about it" gives you a tremendous competitive advantage.

How to make scripts your own

For many years, the concept of scripting what to say has had a negative association in many people's minds. This is because they associate scripting with the telemarketer who calls at dinnertime and is obviously reading directly from a script that has not been made their own.

But making this association is like asking a five-year-old child to read one of Shakespeare's sonnets and then thinking you don't like the sonnet because of the way it was communicated.

It is absolutely imperative that you ultimately make any script you write *your own*.

There are certain words that seem natural to some people and unnatural to others. I recently received a telemarketing call where the caller really said to me, "Yo, is the man that makes the business decisions around?" To which I responded, "Who is asking?" He said, "We have got a special offer on commercial financing for the business owner with a special rate of prime plus zero." He hesitated as he read the lines of the script and it was obvious he wasn't sure what he was talking about. As a result, he immediately lost his credibility with me.

Compare this with another telemarketer who called me, and who was also reading from a script. But she was well rehearsed and comfortable with it. She began, "Hello, Mr. Magnacca. My name is Chris and I am calling you from Citibank. As one of our best customers, I am calling to make you an exclusive offer only available to certain card members. Do you have a moment for me to tell you about it?"

I said, "Yes."

She continued, "We are offering through a special partnership with AT&T a 5-cents-a-minute long-distance package with no contract to sign."

I responded with my well-rehearsed script: "I appreciate your call, but I am under agreement with another carrier for the next year."

She politely responded, "I understand. We'll check back with you at the end of the year."

While she did not close the sale, she succeeded in engaging me in a conversation that I never would have had if she had begun the statement by saying, "Yo, I'm calling about switching your long-distance service."

Using a script gives you the opportunity to both anticipate your response to a likely question and then document the phrases and responses that have worked for you in the past, so you can leverage this knowledge.

The fact is that all of us use a script of some sort every day. Anyone that doesn't consciously organize their thoughts and words would likely suffer from a condition psychologists call "glossalalia," or "word salad," in which random words are uttered without any meaning or connection to each other, such as, "House, up, toothpick, wire cutters."

All of us probably had times in our lives when it felt like we were making no sense with our words, but there usually is some basic organization to our speech.

Clearly, that organization is vital if you are going to script an effective Elevator Speech.

How to craft your Elevator Speech

I once presented a series of marketing seminars to small-business owners who were customers of Staples, and the project gave me a great deal of experience working on Elevator Speeches. One of the most amazing revelations I had was how relevant the concept of an Elevator Speech is to almost any businessperson.

In the course of presenting these seminars for three years, I had the opportunity to meet more than 3,000 small-business owners who represented almost every imaginable industry, from landscape architects to funeral directors, from ambulance service operators to real estate agents.

I would begin the seminar by asking people their names and what business they were in. Inevitably, people would refer to the commodity aspect of their business: "My name is John, and I am in the computer business." "My name is Jane, and I am in the real estate business." As discussed in Chapter Two, I noticed that most people were not communicating the real value they brought to their business or any unique aspects about themselves or what they did.

The Elevator Speech "opener"

I met a participant named Floyd at one of these seminars, who told me he was an automotive consultant. I was unsure what he meant, so I asked him if he was a consultant to the major auto manufacturers.

"No."

"Do you consult to the local franchises?"

"No."

Somewhat exasperated, I finally asked, "What do you really do?"

"Do you know how most people don't like the process of buying a new car because they don't like dealing with the salesperson?

I said, "Yes."

"Well, what I do, for $295, is I take people through a 15-point process designed to help them determine the exact right car for them, and then I go with them to the dealership to negotiate the best price."

As soon as he finished speaking, a woman who was sitting behind him tapped him on the shoulder and said, "Can I have one of your cards?"

There was an electrical charge in the room. It was as if everyone knew he did something unique. I asked him to say it again, and this time I wrote it down. Then, just before the seminar ended, I asked another seminar participant if she remembered what business Floyd was in.

She said, "Oh, sure. What he does is, for $295, he takes you though a 15-point process to help you determine the best car for you to buy and then he goes with you to the dealership to help you buy the car."

This was an "Aha!" moment for me. Floyd said, "I never used this technique before because nobody ever asked me what I really do. Now that I think about it, I'll bet that many of the people I've told I was an automotive consultant misunderstood what I do."

Since that time, I have shared Floyd's approach with advisors around the country and found it to be consistently effective.

Floyd captured the attention of his listeners in a way that was not only easily understood but, more importantly, helped him grow his business through referrals.

The formula behind the strategy Floyd used so effectively can be used by your business as well.

Let's look at exactly what he did.

The first thing he said was "Do you know how . . .?." followed with "Well, what I do is . . ."

There is a great deal of power in using this approach, even though some people may find it a little awkward at first. To those of you who are immediately thinking that you want to modify this strategy, I have this suggestion: Try using this model until you have an Elevator Speech that sticks. It usually takes at least three revisions of any Elevator Speech before you create one that is compelling. Using this structure is the fastest way to get going.

Timing is Everything

There is another benefit to using this strategy that has to do with context and timing. Some people believe that any direct question ("What do you do?") should only be answered with an immediate direct answer ("I am in computers.") However, by using this approach, you are given a moment to think and set up the appropriate psychic real estate—the words, pictures and feelings you want people to associate with your product or service.

By asking the rhetorical question, "Do you know how most people don't like the process of buying a new car, because they don't like dealing with a sales person?" Floyd used the psychological concept called "the undeniable truth." He was offering a statement that almost everyone could agree with, and it had the natural effect of causing people to nod their heads in agreement.

This strategy, which is also referred to as "pacing your audience," is used by virtually every great communicator, from presidents to entertainers. What it does is help create a context where people are signaling that they are in agreement and are willing to listen to what Floyd said next. This paved the way for him to deliver the punch-line: "Well, what I do is . . ."

The simple fact is that fully 50% of the time people are not mentally engaged in what you are saying until you grab their attention. The Elevator Speech opener acts like a hook to grab their attention before you deliver your punch-line. If they don't understand your opening statement, or don't agree with it, then it is unlikely they will understand or respond to whatever you were going to say as a punch-line.

Over the years, I have seen this model used successfully in literally hundreds of businesses across multiple industries. I encourage you to develop two or three versions of your Elevator Speech. First, develop one for people within your industry and use it to clarify what you really do. Second, develop a "layman's version" for people outside your industry. Think of this version as the one you would use during Thanksgiving when distant relatives ask you, "So what business are you in now?" The third version would be a specific Elevator Speech to be used with your primary target market.

For example, if your primary target market is business owners, your third Elevator Speech would probably start like this: "Do you know how most business owners . . .?"

Even if your listener has no need for your product or service, if they can remember what you do, there is always a chance they will know someone to whom they can refer you. (We will talk more about the referral process later in Chapter 6)

I received an e-mail from a management consultant who told me that after completing his Elevator Speech in our seminar program, he went home and practiced it with his 13-year-old daughter. She told him it was the first time she ever really understood what her father did at work, and this provided him with great satisfaction.

After you start using your Elevator Speech, you will wonder why it took you so long to start using one.

The Elevator Speech Generator

Here are some questions to answer to help you generate your own elevator speech:

What are the three primary concerns your clients face?

1.

2.

3.

What are the three things you do to address their primary concerns?

1.

2.

3.

For Example

Primary   Concerns Advisor Actions

Retirement= Develop a financial plan and create an

income stream

Market Turbulence= Quarterly portfolio reviews

Taxes=   Tax planning

Take the information you completed and input it into this format: (use the concerns and actions that are most relevant and compelling for your prospect)

Do you know how….(Insert one primary concern)

What I do is… (Insert what you do to address concern)

Do you know how so many people are worried about whether or not they will be able to retire?

Well, what I do help them create a comprehensive four step financial plan to insure they have an income for the rest of their life.

The goal is for your prospect to say: Really? How do you do that? With this question from your prospect, you have permission to give them additional information.

Elevator Speech Advisor Examples:

Advisor Example 1:

Do you know how many people are feeling confused by all the volatility in the stock market?

Well, what I do is work with people approaching retirement to create a well thought out plan that allows them to sleep at night regardless of the stock markets daily fluctuations.

Advisor Example 2:

Do you know how many employees who have a 401k are unsure about the best way to allocate their money?

Well, what I do is present financial education seminars designed to help people make the best decisions for their retirement.

Advisor Example 3:

Do you know how 50% of small businesses fail in their first five years?

Well, what I do is help my small business clients to manage their assets and liabilities so they can focus on running their business and be in the 50% that succeeds after 5 years.

Advisor Example 4:

Do you know how most business owners are so busy running their business that they do not have time to manage their capital needs?

Well, my team and I work as specialists to business owners providing solutions in the areas of: Retirement, Banking, and Investments to help increase their bottom line profit.

Advisor Example 5:

Do you know how many investors have lost a lot of money in the stock market lately?

Well, what I do is take my clients through a four-step recovery process to help them restore their financial health.

Advisor Example 6:

Do you know how most companies have a CFO to manage their finances?

Well, what I do is work as a personal CFO for business owners and executives to help them focus on what they do best!

Advisor Example 7:

Do you know how so many good people when their employer went bankrupt lost their life savings.

Well, what I do is help my clients to diversify using our four step process to help make sure this never happens to them.

How to hit a hole-in-one

My client, a top-producing financial advisor, was going out to play a round of golf with a friend and had just been introduced to the other two members of his foursome, both business owners. As they were waiting for their bags to be brought around, one of the business owners said to Financial Advisor Frank, "So what do you do?"

Frank said: **"Do you know how most business owners have a CFO to help them manage their company's money?"**

The business owner said, "Yes."

"Well, what I do is work as a personal CFO for my clients to help them make *work optional.*"

The business owner then responded, "How do you do that?"

Just then the golf bags arrived. Frank said, "I would be glad to tell you more about it after the game, but for now let's enjoy the golf."

Frank smiled to himself as he got into the golf cart. He realized that the exact situation he had rehearsed and prepared for had just happened. He was beaming with confidence, because he had said exactly what he wanted to say without sounding scripted.

This was a dramatic improvement over his previous Elevator Speech: "I'm in the life insurance business." That answer typically produced a momentary look of panic on the recipient's face as they began to back away.

Frank called me from the car on his way home from golf. "I can't believe how well this worked," he said. Both of the business owners ended up giving him their cards after the game, and asked that he follow up with them.

Think about the improved psychic real estate Frank created using this Elevator Speech versus what he used to say.

While this Elevator Speech sounds simple, it took us about three hours of work to create it. We needed to understand that Frank's target market was people who owned businesses. They didn't want to fully retire, but wanted work to be optional.

With this knowledge, we helped Frank craft his Elevator Speech and then rehearsed it several times until he could say it naturally and spontaneously. Frank told me he couldn't wait to use it again, now that he had gotten the hang of it.

Tonality and message

A critical component in human communication is the use of *tonality*—the emphasis you give certain words or phrases through the tone in which you speak. When you change your tonality, you fundamentally alter the meaning of what you say.

As you can see from the graph below, the tonality you use accounts for 38% of your overall communication, according to research conducted at UCLA.

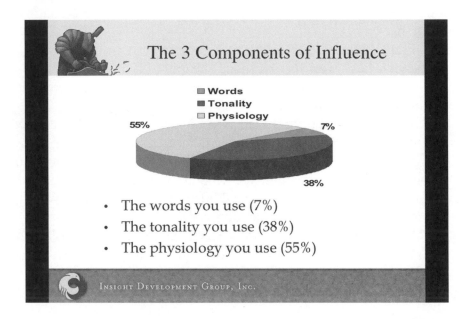

It isn't enough to make sure you say the right words. It's also important that you know *how* to say the right words. Try saying the following sentence out loud, emphasizing the italicized words in each sentence.

- *I* did not say she broke the glass.
- I *did not* say she broke the glass.
- I did not *say* she broke the glass.
- I did not say *she* broke the glass.
- I did not say she *broke* the glass.
- I did not say she broke *the glass*.

Notice how the same sentence can mean so many things depending upon how you say it. The top performers I have studied are masters at using tonality to communicate a point.

The Power of the Pause

There is one other point to make about this. As you watch great speakers communicate with their audience, notice how effectively they use pauses. Top advisors also use the power of the pause in their client interviews and presentations. Strategic pausing allows you to set up your next statement and distinguishes the specific point you want to make.

What not to do

Everything up until now has been designed to show you the best way to get your message across. Sometimes, the best way to understand what to do is to learn what not to do. Sub-par performers act like the person you are about to meet.

No thanks. I'm just looking

How many times have you walked into a retail establishment and, as a salesperson approached, you knew in advance what script he was going to use? As he approached you, 80 percent of the time I bet you heard, "Can I help you?" To which you probably responded, "No thanks, I'm just looking." I've even said that when I really needed help.

What I discovered is that "No thanks, I'm just looking" is a script. It is a rehearsed response to a question we know we are likely to be asked. You may not even be aware that you do this, but the fact is that most of us do.

But what if the retail clerk asked you a different question? What if he said, "Is this your first time in the store?" or "Did you know we are having a sale today?"

All of a sudden, "No thanks, I'm just looking" doesn't work. The new question literally interrupts your pattern of thinking and requires you to answer the question without a scripted response. Your ability to interrupt people's internal dialogue long enough to get their attention makes a big difference in your effectiveness as a communicator.

Many advisors are dismissed before they get a first appointment because people are responding to them the same way many people respond to a sales clerk at the mall.

Here is an example of a salesman who destroyed rapport with two seriously interested prospects in less than five minutes because he didn't understand the power of scripting and tonality.

My wife and I stopped at a Volkswagen dealership to look at the convertible VW Bug. My wife had always liked this car and was thinking she might like to purchase one. Shortly after we entered the dealership, a salesperson approached us and said, "Can I help you?" Like an automaton, I replied, "No thanks, we're just looking."

As we wandered around the dealership for a few more minutes, the salesman came back and asked, "Are you interested in the convertible?"

This was a much better question to ask. I replied, "Yes, my wife is interested in this car."

But rather than directing his communication to my wife, he continued talking directly to me and said, "Are you interested in the 6-cylinder or the 4-cylinder?"

I looked at my wife. She said, "I don't know yet."

I said, "We would like to take the car for a test drive."

With a condescending tonality, the salesman asked my wife, "Do you know how to drive a standard stick car or do you need an automatic?"

She smiled and said clearly, "I can drive a stick, thank you very much."

As we walked outside to get into the car, the salesman said "Before you take the car out, are you planning to buy this car today?" My wife and I simultaneously broke out in laughter. The salesman was taken aback wondering what the joke was.

I looked at him and said, "How could you ask us if we are ready to buy the car today when we haven't even driven the car yet?" He shrugged his shoulders, demonstrating that he had no idea why he had asked the question. It was just part of the script he had been taught.

My wife said to me, "I don't think this dealership is for us. Let's go." As we turned and walked back towards our car, he was left in the awkward position of chasing us down. "Really, you can drive the car, even if you don't want to buy it," he pleaded. As soon as we got in our car, I thought to myself, how tragic it is that so many transaction-based salespeople don't realize the world has changed and they must also change—or suffer the consequences.

The key difference between transactional salespeople and advisors in almost any business is the ratio of asking questions first before making assumptions about what people want or need. Having a powerful opening question you have rehearsed enough to ask naturally is a key factor in positioning yourself properly.

In addition, when I said, "The car is for my wife," picking up on this cue would have helped him avoid destroying rapport with us by ignoring my wife, who was going to make the buying decision. Intriguingly, what bothered us most about the salesman wasn't what he said but how he said it. It's a great reminder of how important it is to be aware of the message you are sending with your tonality.

Something else?

Here is another example where a change in the script and tonality made a positive difference. There is a major coffee chain on the East Coast that used the following script when a customer walked in to order a coffee and donut. The person behind the counter would automatically say, "Is that all?" And they would generally say these words in a particular tone that came across with an edge. The net result was that it sounded like they were telling you that you have had enough, which didn't inspire you to purchase anything else and made you feel unwelcome in the process.

This chain hired a sales psychologist to analyze their processes, and after about an hour of observing the interaction between the staff and customers, he made a simple recommendation. He told the owner that starting the following morning, all of his staff needed to replace the words "Is that all?" with "Something else?" He instructed them to say the phrase with their tone rising on the word "else," making the statement an opening to continue rather than a closing remark. The results of this change were immediate and significant.

First, the owner realized that he had not provided his employees with any direction regarding the most important aspect of their job: How to interact with customers.

Second, he realized that as a result of this, a standard operating procedure had been adopted, not because he had created one, but rather because the newer people were modeling the behavior and language patterns on the employees who had been around for a while.

Perhaps most importantly, he was able to document a measurable increase in the size of his average sale, which he could only attribute to the fact that his staff was now consistently asking if customers wanted "something else?"

He went on to modify the script by having his staff ask customers if they would like to try a "new combo" before saying the new standard of "something else?"

What happened at the donut shop is as relevant for a service business as it is for one that manufacturers products because so many business transactions are based on the same questions that come up over and over again. Whether a financial advisor is being asked, "How do you get paid?" or "What is your investment philosophy," the same questions are asked repeatedly.

Having a clear, prepared answer can help enormously.

Do national companies use this strategy? You bet they do! When you go to a Wendy's, regardless of what you order, they ask "Would you like to super-size it?" In most cases, people say yes.

Tying all the lessons together

Even Fortune 500 companies that are listed on the New York Stock Exchange need to develop an Elevator Speech to communicate what they do in less than 30 seconds in a compelling and memorable way. Here is an example from an actual commercial run by the New York Stock Exchange.

The President of BMC Software is being interviewed about what his company does:

Announcer: "We are here at the New York Stock Exchange with CEO Bob Beauchamp of BMC Software, the largest company in the world totally dedicated and focused on systems management."

Beauchamp: "BMC is able to manage from the network, through the hardware, through the databases all the way up to the end-user experience. Our culture is built on being part of our customer's environment. When our customers are down, BMC is awake and working on it. That's what we do every day. That's all we do."

Announcer: "On the Internet . . . "

Beauchamp: "The Internet era has ushered in a new wave of need for systems management. Today all the Global 2000 companies are worried about what their end-users see."

Announcer: "On moving to the New York Stock Exchange . . . "

Beauchamp: "It reconfirms to our shareholders that we are a powerhouse software company. It sends the right signals to our stockholders, to our employees, that BMC is the quiet giant that is here to stay."

Announcer: "The New York Stock Exchange. The world puts its stock in us."

The commercial ends with the familiar "ding, ding, ding" of the New York Stock Exchange opening bell.

What you may notice in this script is how the words are carefully chosen to send a specific and clear message about what this company does in 30 seconds. When Bob Beauchamp says, "It reconfirms to our shareholders that BMC is a powerhouse software company," the inference is that everyone already knows this, and being listed on the Big Board simply "reconfirms" it.

Your opening and closing script with clients should be as carefully thought out and succinct as the NYSE commercial. Your ability to deliver it with the right tonality will determine whether or not you "ring the bell" with your clients.

The power of listening

Now that we have spent all this time figuring out what to say, you can free your mind up to practice the art of listening.

The biggest difference I have found between a stockbroker and a true advisor is the amount of time they spend listening rather than talking. Stockbrokers are trained to talk first to control the conversation and then listen for buying signals. Advisors are trained to listen first and then diagnose the situation. Only then do they start talking.

Imagine you're sick, and you go to the doctor. Shortly after the doctor greets you, he says, "I have a prescription that I think will help you without making any effort to understand what is wrong." If that were to happen, the doctor would likely lose his credibility immediately.

There are many people who used to be traditional stockbrokers or insurance agents who changed the title on their business cards to "financial advisor" or "financial consultant" without making any change in the way they communicate with clients. As an advisor, not only do you need to listen to the words people use. More importantly, you need to listen to what they are really communicating. Sometimes what they don't say is as instructive as what they do say. The tonality and body language they use can also speak volumes.

I remember having a conversation with a husband and wife in their mid-70s about their estate-planning goals. As I began to ask questions, I discovered there was a problem between my clients and their daughter-in-law. They didn't come out and tell me this in so many words. Instead, it was communicated with facial expressions and tonality. I recognized that even in the context of being a financial advisor in a confidential setting, they were still uncomfortable saying out loud what I felt they were thinking.

As I practiced reflective listening, which is simply repeating back to them my understanding of what they had said, I asked, "Are you concerned that if your son and his wife split up, she will get half of the money you were thinking about giving to him and your grandchildren?" They both immediately nodded their head in agreement. I explained that there was a way to structure a trust to make sure the money they wanted to give ended up either with their son or their grandchildren. As a look of relief washed over their faces, I realized that I would not have been able to discern this information by any other means other than through focused listening.

One of the common denominators I find among the top advisors I coach is their intuitive understanding of the importance of not rushing the fact-finding process. There are some things you cannot shortcut, and listening to what is really being said is one of them. Being a good listener is an attribute that you can develop. Think about the last time in your own life someone really listened to you and gave you their undivided attention.

I'd like you to answer the following questions by reading them out loud to yourself:

1. If there are twelve 1-cent stamps in a dozen, how many two-cent stamps are there in a dozen?_____
2. Some months have 31 days, some 30. How many have 28?_____
3. Do they have a Fourth of July in Canada? _____
4. The farmer had 17 sheep. All but 9 died. How many were left? _____
5. How many animals of each species did Moses take aboard the Ark? ___

Did you answer 12, all of them, yes, 9, and none (it was Noah who took the animals on the Ark, not Moses)?

What this test demonstrates is that we have a tendency to assume what something means even before the thought has been completed. The problem here is that we effectively stop listening once we think we understand what has been asked and start processing the information for an answer. If you answered 2 to question No, 5, that's because your brain focused on the Ark and did not catch that the question asked about Moses, not Noah.

As you think about your own client interaction, rate yourself on a scale of 1 to 10 as to how effectively you listen to what people say. If you feel you need improvement, one helpful strategy is to repeat back what you understood the person to have said and then clarify your understanding. Just as the "Do you know how . . .?" question in the Elevator Speech gives you some "mental oxygen" to think about your next step, the same dynamic is true as you practice reflective listening.

One last point

If you've really been listening to your clients, one of the things you may have noticed is how offensive the word "but" can be. Many relationships get off to a bad start because the advisor unwittingly destroyed rapport by saying "but" instead of "and."

When you say to somebody, "I agree with you, but this is what I think we should do," you have the effect of negating what they just said, and people instinctively are offended by this. It is usually said with only the best of intentions, but nevertheless it causes a communication gap. Notice the difference by changing the phrase and saying "I agree with you, and what I suggest is . . . " Using this strategy, you can still make your point without offending the listener, whether it is your client, boss, spouse, etc.

Takeaway Lessons

- **Very few advisors are willing to invest the time and energy to create, practice and master their Elevator Speech and other scripts**. That's good for you. It will give you an edge.
- **Develop more than one script.** A script that works in one place (talking to colleagues) won't work in another (meeting prospective clients). That's why you need to develop multiple scripts.
- **Remember Floyd.** In constructing your speech, follow the approach he took. It will work wonders.
- **And as long as you are remembering** . . . remember to listen.

"It takes about three weeks to prepare a good impromptu speech"
Mark Twain

Knowledge Application

1. Think about three purchases you have made that involve a salesperson in the past 12 months. How would you rank them as far as technique and why?

2. Develop at least three Elevator Speeches. It generally takes at least three different iterations to create an Elevator Speech that is succinct and effective. Remember to start with an undeniable truth and then continue your response with "Well, what I do is . . . "

Brainstorm with two or three of your peers about several possible answers to the "Do you know how . . .?" question.

3. What are some undeniable truths in your business that most people would agree with? Add them to the "Do you know how" phrase. In other words, ask "Do you know how . . .?" and explain a frustration or pain that your client has. Then tell him, "Well, what we do is . . ." and then solve the client's frustration with your explanation.

4. Think about the psychic real estate you are trying to create in the mind of your prospects or clients. Add this story or metaphor to the "Well, what I do is . . . " phrase.

Chapter 4

Fishing Where the Fish Are

You've got to find them to catch them!

What's ahead in this chapter:

The biggest problem advisors face in finding new prospects is not understanding exactly who they are looking for. What you need is the equivalent of a fish-finder, a form of sonar for fisherman.

Just as a fish-finder lets a fisherman see where the fish are, you will see the best way to seek out the right clients for your business by using your database.

This new way of discerning information will allow you to see patterns and connections that were previously invisible

The fish-finder

The greenish-blue water of Cape Cod Bay was shimmering in the afternoon sunlight as our boat glided along. My father and I had been casting on the surface for striped bass. After about fifteen minutes, without even a nibble, I began to wonder if there were even any fish around. I asked my father why he thought we weren't having any luck and he pointed to the fish-finder he had recently purchased.

A fish-finder produces an image on its screen using sonar, which shows what's underneath your boat. Specifically, it shows the outline of the ocean floor and any schools of fish swimming between your boat and the bottom of the sea. It shows individual fish as a dot on the screen and schools of fish as a cluster of dots.

I had been opposed initially to my father's use of the fish-finder because I thought the technology would take some of the "sport" out of "sport-fishing."

But as my father explained how the fish-finder worked, I learned about three important pieces of information that I had never considered important when catching fish.

First was the water-temperature indicator. On this particular day, the water was warmer than usual. What this meant is that the bass, which like cold water, most likely would not come to the surface.

Second was the depth indicator. The overall depth of the ocean affected what type of fish we were likely to find. You are not likely to find a giant tuna in 10 feet of water, but you can find schools of striped bass.

Third, using the fish-finder, we could see whether or not there were any fish under the boat. More importantly, we could see whether there were schools of fish or just one or two individual fish.

Using this one instrument, we could synthesize three critical pieces of information and become far more effective in our goal of catching striped bass. What I saw on the screen was several dots indicating fish, at a depth of 10 to 20 feet.

Armed with this new information, I changed my strategy and dropped a special lure into the water that was designed to go down to the appropriate depth. We then increased the speed of the boat and saw the fish-finder illuminate, telling us that some fish were now swimming under our boat. Less than ten seconds later, I heard the sound that every fisherman loves: The clicking of a spinning reel.

As I netted a beautiful striped bass, it dawned on me how looking at information in a new way (finding a new way to search out fish) and adjusting your strategy (fishing where the fish are) can have an immediate and powerful effect on your results.

Learning how to fish on land

In 1991, I had an opportunity to see how this concept worked in my own financial advisory business. I had just started in the business during what was correctly considered a difficult economic climate. I was facing many obstacles, some real and some imagined. Many people were still uncertain about investing, thanks to the 1987 stock market crash, and now the real estate market in New England was dropping as well.

During this down period, I was visited by a mutual fund wholesaler named Nick.

When Nick walked in, he immediately sensed that I was having a difficult time in my business because of the grim look on my face.

When he asked, "Who is your target market?" I realized that I didn't really have one. I thought it was anyone who had money and a pulse.

Nick asked, "What happens when you speak to the people you are presently calling?"

"Mostly they hang up."

He laughed and said, "So why do you keep calling these people?"

"I don't really have anything else to do."

Nick chuckled as he asked me, "Why would they want to talk to you? In other words, what value do you bring to the table for them?"

I had no compelling answer to this question, but it did set off a chain reaction that got me thinking about the value I wanted to offer my clients.

What made Nick's approach unique was that he didn't just start talking about the mutual fund products he offered, but rather began to ask me a series of specific questions. In retrospect, I realized these questions were designed to help me focus on whom I should be targeting. With each question he asked, I realized why I lacked confidence in talking to prospects. It was because I was unclear about what business I was in and what I was really selling.

Among the many things Nick said that stuck in my mind was this: "Mark, you've heard the saying that if you give a man a fish you will feed him for a day, but if you teach him to fish, you will feed him for a lifetime? Well I have an addition to that philosophy: You need to start fishing where the fish are."

At first I didn't really understand what he meant, but after I thought about it, I realized that maybe the reason I wasn't catching anything was because there were no fish where I was fishing.

A few days later, an article appeared in *The Boston Globe* that said Massachusetts was going to close 11 state mental hospitals and turn the patients over to private facilities. One of the hospitals to be closed was right down the street from my office. I immediately thought this might be an opportunity to help a large number of people who needed to make important financial decisions in a short period of time. No, not the patients. I wasn't sure I could do much for them. But maybe I could help the people who worked at the facility.

I walked into the hospital and introduced myself to the director of human resources. I asked him what he thought the impact of the state's decision would be on the people who worked for him. He was clearly distressed when he told me that he would have to lay off his entire staff within 90 days. He went on to say that many of his employees had questions about the state pension and their deferred compensation plans, in light of the pending layoffs.

I mentioned that my company conducted financial education seminars and perhaps we could help. The director said he was open to the idea, but that whoever spoke to his group would have to be an expert in three areas: the state pension plan, Section 457 Deferred Compensation Plans, and 403B Plans. I told him I would do some research and get back to him.

After making a few calls to the state retirement board and several 403B plan sponsors, I realized we could help him and his staff with this challenge. I researched and studied all three of the areas he mentioned to me, so I felt confident that I could answer any questions that were likely to arise. Part of my studying included contacting experts in the field to understand what my prospective clients really needed to know. This whole process took me just over two weeks.

I followed up with the HR director to tell him I would be the speaker and showed him my proposed seminar information. He was impressed with the presentation I had created in such a short period of time and gave me a thumbs-up to proceed. At the end of the first seminar, which had 60 attendees, 40 people came up to our small metal card table to sign up for their personal consultation to help them make a decision about what to do. We later held the seminar for the other two shifts. One of the nurses told me word had spread that it was a good seminar and worth attending.

As a result of this seminar, I asked the HR director if he could introduce me to his colleagues at the other 10 state hospitals that were scheduled to close. He wrote a brief letter of recommendation on my behalf, which I sent to the other 10 directors. Over the course of the next six months, I presented this seminar in every one of those hospitals with virtually no competition, because no one else knew there were fish here.

I believe that the insight I received from Nick about fishing where the fish are was partly responsible for my decision to take action and begin marketing to the state hospitals. As a result of this decision, we helped more than 100 people with their financial plans and generated in excess of $10 million in new mutual fund sales— during a time when the market was down and the economy was in a recession.

Don't fish for yesterday's fish

One of the things I learned from my experience at the state hospitals was to avoid fishing for yesterday's fish. Many people with years of experience told me that this type of seminar program had been tried before and wouldn't work. What they didn't realize is that market conditions had changed, so what used to be an effective marketing strategy had changed as well. Rookie fisherman often make the same mistake. They will ask an experienced fisherman what lures he used to catch his fish on a given day when the weather conditions were sunny and warm. On the following day, when the conditions have changed to overcast and cool, rookies will still use the same lures that worked on the sunny day. What they don't understand is the perspective of the fish. When conditions are sunny, fish can more easily see a dark lure because it provides contrast against the bright sky. Conversely, on an overcast day, a brighter lure will often be easier to see against the surface of the water.

There are many factors that go into finding and catching the fish you want. The first step that is critical to success is understanding the environment and perspective of the fish you want to catch. The same concept applies today to your prospecting for clients. What worked in the last market cycle is not likely to continue to be relevant or effective. You need to rethink your marketing plan from the perspective of the prospects you are trying to catch.

No hook, No fish

When my son turned four, we bought him his first fishing pole, which came with a special yellow practice lure. The goal was to teach children how to cast the lure and reel it in. After about a day of practicing with the yellow lure, we were ready to go to a local pond and start fishing. As I began to remove the yellow lure to replace it with a "real" lure my son said, "I want to use the yellow lure." I explained that the yellow lure had no hook. My son said, "That's okay. I'll use it anyway." I decided that the best way to explain to him why a hook was important was with my fishing pole. As I reeled in my first small fish on my pole, my son asked, "Why isn't mine working?" I explained again about the hook and he said, "You mean you really can't catch a fish without a hook?" I nodded, and he said, "Okay, I'll take a hook." In that moment, my son helped me to articulate a concept that's stunning in its simplicity but profound in its implication.

Many advisors' marketing plans are like the practice lure. This lure allows them to pretend they are fishing. But because they have no hook, they have no chance of catching a fish. Even if they dragged their "yellow lure" through a school of hungry fish, they wouldn't snag even one. To be an effective marketer, you need to understand what your "hook" is and how to use it.

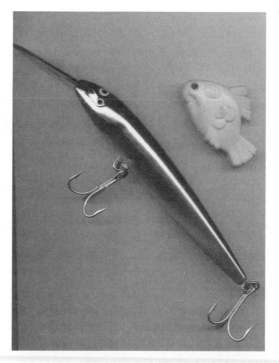

Rapala "Sinking Plongent" Stripped Bass lure and Kids' Practice lure. Which one are you using?

The Science of Pattern Recognition
What do you notice when you look at the figures below.

Write your responses here

1. Did you see a water fountain dripping?
2. Did you see an arrow pointing down?
3. Did you see the word **FLY**

If you didn't see the word FLY at first, this means that you have been conditioned to look for black letters against a white background, just like the pages in this book. It also demonstrates the filter you have in your mind that determines what you see and don't see.

Your "success filter"

Even though you may be getting the right information on your "fish finder," your filter will still determine what you perceive. This filter also determines what opportunities you notice in the marketplace. Without the right filter, an opportunity can be staring you in the face and you won't see it. The first step in this process is recognizing that you have a filter that prevents you from noticing what might be obvious to someone else, like a competitor. By clearly understanding your target market, you begin to notice opportunities that other people miss. I noticed the article in the *Boston Globe* that day, in part because Nick had helped me replace my success filter, which allowed me to notice an opportunity that I may have otherwise missed.

Creating business intelligence

The process of refining data into information and then into knowledge is called **creating business intelligence.** One of the best examples of this process can be found at Amazon.com.

When you visit the Amazon.com Web site, the system immediately recognizes if you are a new or returning visitor. It then welcomes past visitors and says, for example, "Hello, Mark, we have recommendations for you." Those recommendations are based on what you've previously purchased. Then, when you start looking up a book or a CD, the database that powers Amazon will make a recommendation in real time based on what you are looking for. It will say, "If you liked that book, then you may like this book as well."

Never before has there been an ability to sift through so much information so fast and do something meaningful with it.

Here is a sample web page for Amazon.com showing "Your Recommendation."

Many grocery stores also use database marketing to sort out their best customers. After the birth of our son, I wondered why we started getting coupons in the mail for a wide range of baby supplies. I later found out that our local supermarket sells the information it collects on what we purchase with their "discount shopping card." In return for giving us a discount on some products, they sell the information on what we buy to manufacturers who can then refine their target market. In many ways, it's much more efficient and less wasteful for the manufacturers than mass-marketing. The reason that marketers are willing to pay for this data is because it works. We started using the Pampers coupons we received in the mail and soon became loyal customers.

The **bottom line** is that these companies were fishing where the fish are. They targeted the people most likely to use their products.

How can you discern business intelligence from your database? By using "fields" that allow you to sort information and help you grow your business. There are numerous database and customer relationship management programs available in the marketplace. Whether you prefer ACT, FileMaker, Goldmine, Siebel, Salesforce.com or even Microsoft Excel, to name a few, all of these programs allow you to sort and filter information by field.

Fertile "fields"

In the vernacular of database programs, each "box" in which you enter information is called a field. Some fields are numeric and others are text. By breaking information into separate fields, you gain the ability to sort and filter information. For example, when we were conducting educational seminars for doctors, I would first sort our client database by profession, which gave me a list of all the doctors. I could then narrow the look-up to those clients who were doctors in Boston, where we were conducting the seminar. There are several levels of sophistication that you can add to this process by sorting information by field.

To start your database analysis, I recommend you gather the following general information about each of your clients/families: Name, address, date of birth, telephone numbers, fax numbers, e-mail addresses, total assets under management, and revenue per client.

Source of client

In addition, I recommend including a field in the database to indicate the source of the client, whether it was a seminar, personal referral, cold call, advertisement and so on. This will allow you to better understand where your most valuable client relationships are coming from. This is important because it will help you to notice what is already working for you so that you can replicate it.

The ABC's of client management

You can use another field to rank the client as an A, B, or C client, depending on how much business they do—or potentially could do—with you. For some advisors, an "A" client is an individual or family that has at least $1 million of investable assets in their account. A "B" client would be anyone with between $500,000 and $1 million, and a "C" client would be anyone with less than $500,000. You can rank your clients quantitatively any way you want, but it should be done.

In order for the information to be truly meaningful, I have found that it is invaluable to re-sort clients based on their ability to refer you to other clients. In addition, you may want to rank them based on how much you enjoy working with them and how much they seem to appreciate what you do for them. This ranking system helps you determine whether or not you want to continue your business relationship with them based on the value you are providing.

Total-assets field

One of the biggest frustrations clients experience is not receiving an easy-to-read, easily understood financial statement that shows their total portfolio value. Many firms have spent millions of dollars redesigning their brokerage statements to make them more user-friendly. Nevertheless, many clients still complain of not being able to easily understand the total value of what they own at a glance.

In my practice, we had many clients who had investments both in brokerage accounts and other accounts such as fixed or variable annuities. In our database we created a portfolio summary sheet that allowed our clients to view (on one or two pieces of paper) the total value of all their investments regardless of what type of account they were held in.

This cumulative report allowed clients to quickly review the bottom line, giving them a sense of whether they were moving in the right direction. Too often advisors assume that clients review all their separate statements and figure out on their own their total portfolio value. Using a database to update this report makes it consistent, accurate and easier for the client. It also helps you better understand your client's total investment picture, not just the part you manage. The idea of capturing this information may seem basic and obvious, but what I have found is that less than half of the financial advisors I have surveyed around the country use this business intelligence process.

Part of the reason they don't is because many firms store all the relevant information on their clients' portfolios in their internal database system. While these programs provide advisors with access to portfolio numbers, they are generally cumbersome to customize. As a result, I have found that many top performers keep their own client information in a separate database program, like the ones I mentioned earlier, that allows them the flexibility to sort the information in a number of different ways.

You are already a database expert. You just may not have realized it.

I find it interesting that the same quantitative skills advisors use to choose investment managers can be applied to finding the right types of clients. Morningstar is effectively a large database that allows you to sort information on funds to find the right match for your criteria. Almost every advisor has used this tool to help determine whether a particular fund is a match for a client's objective. Virtually all the performance rankings produced by the major investment newspapers and periodicals are sorted databases of information. The raw information is generally not useful for making decisions, but the mosaic of information becomes understandable as a result of the sorting and interpretation of the information you refine. Although this topic can seem complex, the fact is you use powerful databases to sort and filter information every time you look something up on the Internet. If you are comfortable doing that kind of search, you can do this as well.

The 80-20 rule lives!

Several years ago, my accountant introduced me to a "revenue-sorting strategy." What a revelation! He produced a report by creating a field in my database called "Total Revenue Per Client," which included all revenue received in the current year. Before I saw the results, I was confident that I knew who my best customers were. In fact, I would have been willing to bet that I knew off the top of my head not only who they were but where they came from and why they worked with me.

Something startling happened when we tabulated the results. I was wrong! Not just a little wrong, but way off base.

My accountant had told me that in most businesses the "80–20 Rule" is alive and well. The rule says that 80 percent of sales are produced from 20 percent of customers. I remember telling my accountant that while the rule might hold true in most businesses, in my business it was closer to 50–50. He nodded, and said, "Okay, let's look at the numbers."

I couldn't believe my eyes. Almost 90 percent of our revenue had come from 38 clients out of a total of 300. Not only was it not 50–50, it wasn't even 80–20. In fact, it was closer to 90–10: 90 percent of our gross revenue had come from just 10 percent of our clients!

This was a profound realization for me. The next question my accountant asked was, "What are the common denominators among your best customers, these 38 people?" I wasn't sure, but after about five minutes of categorizing each one, I determined that the vast majority of these clients had the following characteristics:

- More than 55 years old
- Received a buy-out package from previous employer
- Came to us after attending a seminar
- Attended that seminar because it was recommended to them by a friend or their employer

We had been spending almost $2,000 a month in advertising in certain periodicals, money that was difficult to justify up to this point. Now that I could see this spending in a new light, the ads were a complete waste of money. I also realized I could create an ideal customer profile that would function just like a lure designed to catch certain fish under certain conditions.

The millionaire demographic

In their book *The Millionaire Next Door,* authors Tom Stanley and William Danko describe their study of where wealth is concentrated in the United States. Their primary tool was the demographic information provided by several different governmental agencies, including the U.S. Census Bureau.

What Stanley and Danko did was to perform a version of business intelligence on the census data. Their conclusion? Many of the people who seem wealthy are not, and many who give no indication of being wealthy are in fact the millionaires who live next door.

It would be easy to assume that people who live in wealthy suburbs in expensive houses and drive luxury cars are in fact wealthy. As they performed some business intelligence on their data they began to notice a fascinating pattern. There were many people who had high incomes and virtually no "real" wealth because they consumed their income as quickly as they earned it.

By contrast, there was another group whom they called "prodigious accumulators of wealth." This group had as a common denominator frugality, which is not a trait you typically associate with being wealthy. Their frugality caused them to stay in the same house even after they could afford to move to a more expensive one. It typically made them shop at J.C. Penny rather than Brooks Brothers, and drive a car that was a few years old, rather than a brand-new one.

This research has helped many advisors rethink their demographic target market. For example, many financial advisors have made the assumption that marketing to "high-income professionals" was the right choice for them, only to find out that this group often has very little discretionary income or investable assets.

Your natural market

After you have completed your database analysis and determined the common denominators of your best clients, you may notice that they are all part of a certain "natural market." Your natural market is usually a group of people with whom you have a natural affinity. An obvious example is the F-14 pilot I mentioned earlier who targeted his marketing efforts to retired military officers. He has a natural advantage in this market because he understands what matters to these people on a personal level.

A less obvious example occurred after I did my database analysis and noticed that three of my top ten clients were in the fuel oil distribution business.

Before I met my first client in this business, I had no affinity to this group whatsoever, except that I had pumped a lot of gas as a consumer. As I developed a deeper relationship with my first client, I began to understand some of the unique challenges he faced because he worked in a family business. After I was introduced to the association he was part of, he referred me to two other business owners (who weren't competitors because they covered different areas). As I began to work with the two referrals, I recognized that much of what I had learned that mattered to my first client was also important to these prospects. I was able to attain the role of trusted advisor in both cases much faster because of what I had learned working with the original client.

The bottom line is that after working with these three clients, I had developed a new "natural market" for myself, because I understood the issues and challenges they faced and the best solutions for dealing with them.

Sometimes it is easy to overlook a natural market because it seems so obvious. One of my first marketing efforts was focused on educators at the high school and college level. I felt very comfortable with this group, in part because my mother was a teacher, and I understood many of the issues that faced educators.

Using your database to determine your service level agreements

There is a considerable distinction between transactional businesses and fee-based businesses in terms of the need for some type of Service Level Agreement (SLA). An SLA is an agreement that defines what kind of service each client can expect from you. For example, in the airline business, passengers who pay for a first-class ticket expect a different level of service than passengers in coach. They board and de-plane first, they receive "better" meals and wider seats, and their movies are free. There are many people who can afford a first-class ticket but would never think to purchase one because they don't value the additional services as worthy of the price tag.

This is an important concept for advisors because many advisors set expectations to deliver first-class service but charge coach fares. In order to determine what you are really being paid on a per-client basis, you need to look not only at the revenue but also at the time you spend with a given client.

Here's an example. One of my coaching clients, Greg, had two clients he wanted to talk to me about. One had $40 million invested with him and the other had $4 million.

Greg was splitting the fee he received from his $40 million client with two other advisors and spending 8 to 10 hours a month on him. His $4 million client, on the other hand, paid Greg almost the same amount in gross fees as his *pro rata* share from the $40 million client. However, he only required one or two hours of attention per month for him to feel he was receiving excellent service.

After he reviewed these numbers, Greg decided that he needed to implement a Service Level Agreement. He recognized that while providing excellent service was important to all of his clients, it was not cost effective for everyone with whom he worked.

Still, he was concerned that providing anything less than 110% service level to his clients would be a problem.

I worked with him to develop a script that allowed him to communicate what is included as part of his client experience for his standard 1% fee. Clients who needed work outside that scope would simply pay for it on an hourly basis. In addition, I recommended that he complete a communication survey with all his clients to determine what they really wanted. As a result of this survey, he realized that the vast majority of his clients didn't want or need the 25-page quarterly reports he produced for each client. This freed up a huge bottleneck that had been created with his staff, who were spending a large portion of every day preparing these reports for client meetings.

Because Greg is an extremely detail-oriented person, he assumed that all his clients required the same level of detail that he did personally. Understanding that most did not, allowed him to free up the one or two hours he typically spent reviewing each of these reports prior to meeting with his clients. In place of the longer reports, most of his clients opted for a one- to two-page executive summary that gave them an overview of their financial status. This new-found time could now be used for prospecting.

Using the "Net" to find your best fish

Prior to 1995 and the Internet's widespread availability, finding your target fish was a lot more difficult and expensive. Although powerful database programs for sorting people and businesses based on certain criteria have existed for many years, they were often far too expensive for the average person to purchase. Companies like Hoovers and D&B have provided lists for many years, but now much of the same information is not only easy to find, but available for free on the Internet.

After you determine your ideal target prospect, you can begin to sort other attributes they have in common. As I planned my next "fishing trip," I asked my three clients in the fuel oil distribution and gas station business about their industry trade associations. They were all members of the New England Service Station and Automotive Repair Association. I thought other members of this association were likely to face the same problems and challenges as my three clients.

In less than five minutes you can use a search engine to find a directory of associations and use it to find the associations that include your clients among their membership. You can also use Web sites such as www.superpages.com not only to create a map of where your prospects live, but even find the neighbors of your best clients.

Psychographics-understanding why people buy

Have you ever wondered why some fish go for certain lures and other fish don't? For thousands of years, fishermen have tried to figure out what actually motivates fish to bite. Likewise, for the past century, marketers have debated what causes humans to purchase or not to purchase. I believe that the vast majority of buying decisions we make are for emotional reasons, and we then use logic to justify those decisions. Think of a recent purchase you have made and ask yourself, "Was this decision based on emotion or pure logic?" **Understanding the emotions and values that drive the people in your target market is critical in creating your marketing plan and go-to-market strategy.**

The term "psychographics" entered the marketing lexicon in 1965. While there are many complex definitions for this label, in actuality it is simply a creative tool that helps you understand some of the core values that drive different decision-making processes. While many experts have acknowledged the validity of psychographics research, it was very difficult to quantify its effectiveness. This changed as a result of a groundbreaking research study from Stanford University called The Values and Lifestyle Survey (VALS). This survey made psychographics' information usable for marketers. Just as demographic research focuses on *where people live*, psychographics research focuses on *why people buy*.

The survey results broke the consumer population down into eight segments based on responses to the VALS questionnaire. Each category of people had different values that motivated their buying decisions. (The full research is available from the Stanford Research Institute at www.sric-bi.com.)

The best way to demonstrate the predictive power of the psychographics is to show you how accurately it can predict human behavior. For example, if you happened to look out of your office window while waiting for a client, and you saw him or her drive up in a late-model Volvo station wagon with a baby seat and a "Save the Seals" bumper sticker, you would probably make certain assumptions about what they value.

What if they drove up instead in a Ford pickup truck with a shotgun rack in the back window and an NRA bumper sticker? How different would your assumptions be about what this person values?

(By the way, the psychographic research is frequently used in national advertising campaigns, whether it be Volvo ads featuring safety, which is very high in value for Volvo's target audience, or Ford ads featuring American flags and showcasing its American heritage, which is very important for Ford's target audience.)

Each of these pieces of information—the Volvo, the baby seat, the bumper sticker—is like a piece of a puzzle. Taken alone, they aren't really clear. However, when put together with all the other pieces, a clear picture emerges of your target clients.

Once you have figured out what you are fishing for and what attracts these fish, the process of fishing becomes an exciting adventure rather than an exercise in frustration.

Takeaway Messages

- **Sort your clients by revenue.** This will help you determine who your most important relationships are.
- **Survey your clients to determine whether a Service Level Agreement makes sense for your practice.** Explain what is included in your fee structure. They will pay for the service level they value.
- **Find groups and associations whose members share demographic and psychographic profiles with your best customers.** Then market to them and use the right hook.

"It's not enough to have intelligence, it's the application of intelligence that counts"
Rene Descarte

Knowledge Application

1. List your top five client relationships

2. What was the original source of these relationships? (i.e. cold call, referral, etc.) Be specific

3. What are some of the common denominators of these relationships? (A certain age group, members of a certain club, etc.)

4. What is the most important value to this person? (Family, Security, Achievement, Peace of mind)

5. Why do they do business with you?

Chapter 5

Your Personal IPO (Initial Prospect Offering)

Don't just tell them, show them

What's ahead in this chapter:

To recap, so far we've learned:

How to determine what business you are really in.

What you want your brand to connote.

A succinct and memorable way to articulate what you do.

Which prospects are most likely to respond positively to your value proposition.

But the phone is still not ringing off the hook.

In this chapter you will learn about one more step you need to take to pull everything together. This last step is the creation of your Personal Initial Prospect Offering (IPO) Kit. You will learn what an IPO Kit is and how to use its contents effectively. Your IPO Kit is the lure you will use to attract the fish you want to catch.

The purpose of your Initial Prospect Offering Kit is simple: You want to encapsulate the essence of who you are, and what you do, in a way that is easy for you to distribute and for prospects to understand.

Your IPO Kit typically consists of a two-pocket folder that holds documents that describe you, your company, your investment process and what other people have to say about you.

This IPO Kit can be used in the following ways:

- *In one-on-one meetings with prospects*
- *Mailed ahead before you meet with clients*

- *With strategic partners such as accounting and estate-planning firms*
- *To help create publicity about some aspect of your business.*
- *To create context that gives you permission to tell your story in a compelling way.*

This Personal IPO Kit answers the same type of questions investors have about an initial public offering of a company's shares. In that case investors want to know:

- *The background of the management team*
- *An overview of their market space*
- *The history of the business opportunity*
- *How much funding is required*
- *The expected return on investment*

Your personal IPO Kit is designed to answer similar questions prospects might have about hiring a financial advisor, such as

- *Who are you?*
- *What is your background?*
- *What business are you in?*
- *What makes your offering unique?*
- *Why should I invest with you?*

How do you rate a financial advisor?

When you talk to a client about a mutual fund, you generally mention its Morningstar Fund rating, and you might explain the difference between a four-star fund and a five-star fund. The Morningstar system gives investors a frame of reference for comparing funds.

The problem is that there is no Morningstar rating system for financial advisors. So it is very difficult for clients and potential clients to compare one advisor to another.

This is no small point. Having a rating can be a very powerful thing. Let me give you an example.

I recently wanted to purchase a book on eBay.com. Once I found it, I realized there were several different sellers from whom I could purchase this book for the same price. With just a few clicks of the mouse, I was able to read what other people who had purchased items from these individuals had to say about them and the transaction.

Because I was sending money to somebody I had never met, it was imperative to me that there be some way to validate their character and ability to follow through. The profile eBay created helped me decide whom to purchase the book from.

There are some informal ratings that are extremely valuable from a marketing standpoint if you are fortunate enough to be included. For example, *Worth* magazine features a yearly profile of the "Top 250 Best Financial Advisors in America," who are selected based on nominations from readers, clients, industry associations, investment firms, and other advisors. Candidates submit extensive surveys about their personal backgrounds and their business practices, which are also used as part of the selection criteria. This is an example of a ranking system that is very helpful to prospects trying to filter through the hundreds of advisors in their area.

However, the ranking is limited to 250 people. If you are number 251, you're out of luck.

Another way to distinguish yourself is with some of the more prestigious designations such as Certified Financial Planner (CFP) and Chartered Life Underwriter (CLU). Only 40,000 people out of 650,000 people who call themselves financial planners have earned the CFP title.

But you may not have earned those letters. And even if you have, 39,999 others have too, so you still need to distinguish yourself further.

And the key word there is **you.** You need to do something on your own, and that is where the IPO Kit comes in. My goal for you with your IPO Kit is to help distinguish you from the competition.

101

The timing for creating one couldn't be better.

In February 2003, *Smart Money,* a magazine for do-it-yourself investors, published a cover story on how to find a great financial advisor. The article made it clear that now, more than ever, investors are seeking the advice of financial planners. The good news for investors is that there are 650,000 financial advisors from whom to choose. The bad news is that there is little information available to help private investors distinguish between highly qualified advisors and those who are incompetent.

Think of the significance for you as a financial advisor: One of the most important magazines for personal investors is now saying you *do* need a financial advisor.

Using your IPO Kit will allow you to position yourself correctly and be able to answer the questions *Smart Money* and other leading newspapers and periodicals such as *Business Week* and *USA Today* are suggesting prospective investors ask when searching for a financial advisor. These "due diligence" questions include:

What are your credentials, experience and areas of expertise?
How are you compensated?
Will you provide a comprehensive financial plan or just portfolio advice?
What type of clients do you serve?
Will you be my fiduciary?
Can you give me references from other clients?
Have you ever been publicly disciplined for any unlawful or unethical action?
Can I get a written agreement detailing fees, fiduciary oath, and services to be provided?
How often will you review my financial plan or portfolio with me?
Are you a member of any financial planning or advisor organization?

Dilbert Reprinted by permission of United Feature Syndicate, Inc.

Your IPO Kit can be used to answer most of the questions prospective investors are being told to ask. Some advisors even use a **Frequently Asked Questions sheet** to provide a thoughtful response to the above questions.

Many clients had positive things to say about my IPO Kit, but one client in particular explained why she really appreciated the information I sent her in advance of our meeting. The other two advisors with whom she had met simply gave her a business card and a brochure about their firm. After meeting with me and reviewing my IPO Kit, she realized there were several questions about their backgrounds that she had forgotten to ask. Instead of calling the others back to ask additional questions, she decided to begin working with me because I had given all the information she needed to make a decision.

Creating an IPO Kit helps differentiate you simply because the vast majority of advisors do not have one. And it allows you to bring together everything you have learned thus far in this book.

Your IPO Kit is designed to help you communicate your process and set expectations about what you do. The best way to guarantee a consistent client experience is never to promise more than you can deliver. In your IPO Kit you can let clients know what you are going to do for them and how you are going to do it.

The inside view

Inside your IPO Kit you can use a number of different documents to make the intangible, tangible.

When you think about what causes people to make buying decisions, a large part of the final decision-making process for a prospect usually comes down to "I trust him and I like him."

Often, in initial prospect meetings, there is a high degree of tension because of a previous bad experience with another advisor. When you send your IPO Kit ahead of time, you are creating psychic real estate about who you are and what you do even before you meet the client. This can help to eliminate some of that "first-meeting" tension.

In addition, your IPO Kit functions as an outline to help you present your value proposition in an organized and consistent manner.

As I built my business and realized we had to systematize our process of dealing with prospects and clients, I began carrying a three-ring binder that included a duplicate of all the elements in my IPO Kit I had already given to the prospect. If they had read this information prior to the meeting, I would review it at the appropriate pace with them. If they had not had an opportunity to review it, I would say, "I would like to take a few minutes to walk you through some background on our firm and give you some background information on me. After that, I would like to ask some questions about you. Is that okay?"

Typically the prospect would answer, "Yes, that would be fine." If for some reason he or she said "No," I would then ask, "What are you hoping to achieve by working with a financial advisor?" I would then listen and not say a word until they answered that question. Depending on how they answered, I would respond using an example such as "Well, Mr. Client, if you went to the doctor and said you had a certain pain and you wanted the doctor to help you, but you didn't feel comfortable giving the doctor any additional information, it would be very hard for the doctor to assist you. In the same way, I need to understand your situation in more detail before I can even begin to make any recommendations. Also, just like the doctor, what we discuss today is confidential and will remain confidential unless you give me permission to discuss your situation with other professionals. Does that make sense to you?"

Your personal biography

The personal biography covered in Chapter 2 is one of the foundational elements of your IPO Kit. It is also the one part of the kit that can be used independently. Depending on the audience you are addressing, you can customize your personal biography by highlighting certain elements that are important to a particular group.

I used different versions of my biography depending on whom I was addressing. For example, when presenting a seminar series to a group of employees from a large telecommunications company, I featured elements of my biography that were of particular interest to this target market but would be irrelevant to others. In this case, I had published a series of articles in the company's corporate newsletter on financial planning issues as they related to this group.

Remember that your biography is a "work in progress" and that you should update it at least once a year to reflect any notable changes in your life. For example, when you receive designations such as the CFP, it is important to update both your business card and your biography.

The problem with many of these designations is that the average prospect doesn't know what they mean. People know what M.D. means. Most people don't know the meaning of CFP, CLU, and all the others, so not only do you want to list the fact that you have earned the designation, you'll want to explain the designation.

Several years ago, I was talking with a friend who was a wholesaler for a major mutual fund company, and he told me about an interesting situation. Bill was an advisor who worked for a wirehouse where he had a client who was a local business owner. This client had about $500,000 invested with him and they had a good working relationship.

The client subsequently sold his business for $9 million, and when he was meeting with his CPA, the accountant said that because of the sale, the business owner was now in a different financial category and needed to be working with an advisor who had at least a CFP designation. Not surprisingly, the accountant offered a referral.

The business owner met with the new advisor at the accountant's office and agreed to invest with him and move his funds out of his account with Bill.

A few days later, just before he received the transfer paperwork, the client called Bill and explained why he was leaving. Bill was aghast because he had just completed his CFP after two years of hard work. When he told his client that he also held a CFP designation now, he said, "Why didn't you tell me that?" He replied, "I just got it." The client said, "I'm really sorry, but I've already made a commitment to go with the other advisor."

The moral of the story is that you need to highlight new designations you receive—and are about to receive—and explain what they mean to your clients and prospects. This kind of information can even be sent out by you as a "press release" to your existing clients and the local newspaper. A copy of this press release can then be included in your IPO Kit.

Letters of recommendation

Letters of recommendation are another important addition to your IPO Kit. This is one of the most simple and inexpensive yet powerful tools I can share with you in marketing your business.

Having a third party's written letter of recommendation as a way of introducing you is an idea that has been around for a long time. In fact, it was quite common for young people who were trying to get established in a trade back in the 1700s to carry a letter of recommendation with them. In his autobiography, Benjamin Franklin talks about how the letter of recommendation from the printer to whom he was apprenticed in Boston allowed him to become quickly established when he moved to Philadelphia.

The fact that someone is willing to write a letter on your behalf typically signifies that you are someone in whom they have confidence.

The beauty of using letters of recommendation as part of your IPO Kit is that your clients can say things in the letter that are meaningful to your prospects and that wouldn't necessarily be appropriate for you to say. For example, a client can refer to your abilities, talent and thoughtfulness in a way that would be improper for you to say yourself. No one likes a braggart, but everyone wants to work with someone who comes highly recommended.

One of the biggest questions people ask about letters of recommendation is how you get them. The answer is simple: You ask.

But that is only part of the answer, because you certainly don't ask just once. After I have presented one of my programs to a client—and assuming I have met their expectations, I often ask clients if they would be willing to write me a brief letter of recommendation. In almost every case, they are willing to do it.

The next point will require a degree of subtlety so as not to seem presumptuous. My suggestion is to ask your potential letter writer if you can send them some samples of what other people have written as a model for them to look at. In some cases, people will say, "Why don't you write the letter to give me a frame of reference as to what you are looking for and I will edit it before I sign it?"

In most consulting or advisory businesses, the ability to use these letters as a part of your IPO Kit is incredibly valuable. For Registered Investment Advisors, you typically cannot use outside testimonials, but there are other ways to accomplish the same goal. For example, if you are quoted in the paper or in a newsletter, this can often serve as a third-party endorsement for you.

Printed testimonials

Whether you choose to use the entire letter of recommendation or simply extract one or two sentences to form a printed testimonial, the result is the same: A third-party endorsement of what you do.

One of the benefits of the IPO Kit is that it can be customized for each prospect. I included some documents for everybody and others I inserted into the pockets depending upon the origin of the prospect. For example, if I were meeting a doctor for the first time, I would include letters of recommendation or printed testimonials from other doctors. If the prospect were a business owner, I would include testimonials from other business owners.

Again, this is not new. John Henry Patterson, the founder of National Cash Register, had his salespeople do something similar more than 100 years ago. When one of his salesmen was calling on a grocer, he was required to show the grocer a flyer that had printed testimonials from other grocers. Patterson believed a baker wouldn't believe a testimonial from a butcher.

As much as the world has changed since 1897, the core concept remains the same.

Testimonials are important. In the world of restaurants, a review in the paper by an influential restaurant critic can make or break a new restaurant. Pizzeria Uno understands the power of the printed testimonial. They showcase copies of restaurant reviews from newspapers nationwide in the entranceway of every one of their restaurants. The articles all describe how wonderful their Chicago-style pizza is, and as a consumer you are a lot more likely to believe it from a restaurant critic than from Pizzeria Uno itself.

Think about how many movie advertisements feature testimonials from moviegoers who have just seen the movie, espousing why they liked it. When you go into a bookstore, you'll find a table piled with books on the Bestseller list, which is a way of saying these books are popular with other people, so you may be interested as well. And almost every book has some kind of testimonial on the back cover, written by an influential person talking about why you should read the book.

Advisors can use the same concept because prospects are more likely to believe what another individual like them has to say about the advisor, rather than the words coming from the advisor himself.

One-sheet marketing piece

I recommend using a one-sheet marketing piece that gives prospects an overview on your firm, the type of clients you work with, a list of your services and an explanation of how you get paid. Too often advisors who have transitioned to the fee-based model presume that prospects understand the distinctions between fee-based and transactional compensation structures. As a rule they don't, and it is always a question they are thinking about, even if they don't ask it.

The one-sheet marketing piece can also include a brief overview of your investment philosophy and describe other members of your team. As you can see, a one-sheet overview provides information on your company, similar to the information your biography provides about you.

Article of interest to your prospect

I recommend including a relevant article about a subject that you know your prospect will find interesting. (Remember, you want to customize your IPO Kit for each potential prospect.) All of these pieces, working together, help to create the psychic real estate that you are someone who is not only competent but trustworthy.

This system is designed to help you get in the door and schedule a first appointment. It does not convert the prospect into a client by itself, but it does pave the way for you to give your best presentation.

Publicity

If your IPO Kit contains nothing but your biography, a few letters of recommendation and a one-sheet that explains your product or services, you will be far ahead of your competition. There is, however, one more component that can make a tremendous difference in credentializing what you do, and that is to harness the power of the media. People believe what they read. Your credibility is established immediately when you are quoted as an expert source in a newspaper or a magazine—providing, of course, the quote reflects your intelligence! When dealing with the media it is very important to script exactly what you want to say and beware of extemporaneous "off the record" comments. What you say can be misconstrued and you often have no chance to clarify a misquote until it is in print, and then it is too late. Nevertheless, when you are clear about your message, the media can be extremely effective in helping you disseminate your message to your target audience.

By completing the IPO Kit as I have described, you have already answered many of the questions a journalist would ask if she were interested in writing about you or your company. These questions include:

Who are you?

What is your background?

What do you do?

What do other people say about you?

Why should people care about you or your company?

What makes you different?

While the strategies I will now share can help you generate national publicity in media outlets such as CNN, *USA Today,* or *The New York Times,* for most people it will be more relevant for an article in a local newspaper or industry trade publication.

People often ask me, "How can I generate publicity about what I am doing?" Before you decide how to generate publicity, you need to understand why you want the publicity and how you will use it.

In my own business, I have received as much value from recycling publicity in the form of reprints and mailings as I have from the initial publication. We talked about the power of database marketing in Chapter 4. You can use the same strategy to create a media list of publications and journalists who fit a certain criteria. First, ask yourself, "What do the investment prospects you have targeted read or watch on TV?" Next, how do you create a newsworthy angle about your product or service that will capture the attention of journalists and editors? One of the most innovative ways to do this is to call a reporter from a periodical or newspaper in which you would like to be featured. These people can be valuable resources when determining your most compelling angle.

Hiring a good publicist may be a great investment depending upon the time and money you are willing to devote.

Regardless of whether you hire someone or do it yourself, your IPO Kit will make the process easier for everyone involved.

Best of all, media coverage has a tendency to build on itself. If you start with a small article in a local paper and photocopy it for your kit, you begin to build the credentials that make it easier to attract the interest of larger publications. (Remember to ask about copyright and reprint policies, because newspapers and magazines have different rules regarding use of their material.)

I recommend having reprints made of any articles in which you have been featured or quoted as an expert. This is especially powerful when you are quoted in a trade journal that is read by your target audience, and you have customized your IPO Kit for this target market.

Social proof

People tend to have more faith in what they read than in what they hear. By documenting everything in your IPO Kit, you are leveraging a powerful psychological concept called "social proof." Social proof is an important concept that ties together everything you have learned so far, because it explains how investors make decisions regarding what to do and whom to follow.

In his book *Influence,* Dr. Robert Cialdini, a professor at the University of Arizona, says that social proof is among the most powerful forms of influence on human beings. Social proof means that **when human beings are uncertain about what to do, they tend to look around and do what everyone else is doing.** Clearly, most major stock market manias are the result of people believing that something—be it biotech stocks or technology stocks or tulips—has a certain value based solely upon the idea that it seems like everyone else thinks so too.

There is a famous episode on the old *Candid Camera* television show called "The Elevator." In it, Alan Funt filmed people's reactions as they entered an elevator where they find three people— all *Candid Camera* employees—already in the elevator, facing the back of the car.

Amazingly, in every instance, the unsuspecting subject turns around and faces the wall as well.

The reality is that many investors today feel like the subject in the elevator. They are hearing different messages about whom to trust and what to do. In many ways they continue to be influenced by social proof. Your ability to generate social proof can significantly shorten the time frame required to transform a prospect into a client.

The ultimate form of social proof is word-of-mouth communication from somebody you trust. Why do advertisers hire celebrities to talk about their product? Because they want to leverage that person's reputation and social proof, creating an effect called **trust transference.**

Here's one of my favorite examples.

In the late 1700s a young man was looking to borrow money to finance his new business. The young man decided to start with the Baron de Rothschild, because everyone in Paris knew that he was among the wealthiest men in France.

Every day at 10 a.m., the Baron stopped by the Paris Bourse (the stock exchange) for a brief visit to see how his investments were doing. The young man, knowing Rothschild's schedule, approached the Baron as he was entering the building and explained that he was looking for help to finance his business. The Baron listened as the young man enthusiastically described his plans. As somebody who had spent a lifetime making quick decisions about people's character and their intent, he felt this young man was worth helping.

The young man said, "Would you be willing to invest in me?"

The Baron said "No, but I will help you." As the Baron, who used a walking stick, began to walk into the Bourse, he said to the young man, "Come with me."

The young man held out his arm to help the Baron walk through the hall. In spite of all the noise, everyone saw him with the Baron. As he got to the other side, the young man said, "Are you sure you can't help me?"

The Baron smiled and said, "I just did. You will now be able to get your loan from one of the men inside."

And, of course, the young man did. Rothschild's actions are one example of someone lending his influence. Referrals (which we will discuss in the next chapter) are another.

Takeaway messages

- **Your IPO Kit should include** a personal biography, letters of recommendation, one-sheet marketing piece, press release, publicity materials, and answers to Frequently Asked Questions.
- **A Professional Look.** It is important to make sure that the look and feel of your IPO Kit resonates with your target clients. Most of the major brokerage firms have internal marketing departments that can help you create this IPO Kit. For independent advisors, many broker-dealer firms have people they can recommend even if they do not have the resources on staff. Just as all of the Starbucks have a consistent look and feel designed to attract their target market clients, your IPO Kit should be consistent throughout.
- **Use your professional designation initials (such as CFP) if you have them**. If you don't have them, consider getting those that would be most important to your target market.

"Don't be so humble, you're not that great"
Golda Meir

Knowledge Application

Answer the following questions:

1. Which clients can you ask for a letter of recommendation?

2. When should you ask for the letter of recommendation?

3. Does the design of your IPO kit appeal to your target market prospects?

4. What interesting angle can you use to contact the local media regarding writing a story on you?

Chapter 6

The Referral Process

All Referrals are not created equal

What's ahead in this chapter

We've covered a lot of material in the previous six chapters. Now it is time to explain how this all works together to form a comprehensive personal marketing strategy that leads you to getting more of the right kind of referrals.

I will show you several proven strategies designed to help make the referral process more enjoyable and productive.

The science of generating referrals

Everyone has heard that in order to get referrals, you have to ask for them. So why is it so hard to ask? I believe there are two reasons.

First, there is a self-imposed glass wall, because many advisors are concerned about the possibility of rejection.

Second, most advisors do not have a clear script to follow that will produce the desired result. The most successful referral prospectors are those advisors who are absolutely convinced of the value they bring to the table. They have an enthusiasm about wanting to share what they know and a desire to help.

What I have found in studying some of the best referral prospectors in the business is their excellent timing regarding asking for a referral. While there are many schools of thought on this matter, I think it is inappropriate to ask for referrals before you have done anything to prove you deserve one.

Instead, the first step I recommend in beginning your referral process is to review your database using the ideas covered in Chapter 4 to determine who has given you the most productive referrals to date. These are the people I would begin focusing your attention on.

The reason is simple. All people are not created equal when it comes to giving referrals. There are certain people for whom giving referrals comes easily and others for whom it is very difficult. There are some people whose personality allows them to become convinced about your skill level and competence after just one or two appointments, but such people are the exception. At the other end of the spectrum, there are people you can know for twenty years who trust you implicitly but will still not give you a referral. The vast majority of people fall somewhere in between.

The natural buying cycle

In almost every business, there is a natural buying cycle. Just as many people buy a new car every three to five years, or a new house every five to seven years, there is a natural buying cycle in the financial advisory business. It is no secret that people are most motivated to act when they have to make an important decision related to money. Whether it is the result of receiving an inheritance, selling a business or piece of property, or retiring, there are certain time cycles for seeking financial advice.

The desire and opportunity to give referrals also has a natural cycle. Some of the clients who are unable to offer you a referral today may be able to give you one next week, next month, or next year. Your ability to systematize your referral process will determine your success in this area over the long term.

All that said, there are some people who are disproportionately more likely to refer you. Think of them as referral **centers of influence.** I had a client who was one of those people who seemed to know everyone. After working with her for about six months, she referred me to three members of her family. After that, she invited me to come speak to her investment club. She was like my Baron de Rothschild, because although she never specifically told people they should invest with me, she helped create a context in which it was obvious that I worked with her and that she was satisfied with the results.

But she is the exception. I recommend that you set your referral expectations properly. In my experience, if five out of ten people you ask for a referral actually give you one or more names, then you are doing well. I believe you are setting yourself up for unnecessary frustration if you get angry when some of your clients do not refer you, because their reason for not referring you may have nothing to do with you personally.

The referability test

One of the best ways you can determine whether somebody is going to give you a referral is by asking them the following question (which I call the referability test):

> *"Mr. Client, what is most important to you before you decide to make a referral to your friends or family*

about a product or service you are very satisfied with?"

Depending upon how they answer this question, you will have a tremendous insight into whether they are likely to refer anybody to you or not.

If they struggle as they think about the question, it is reasonable to believe that they probably don't refer products or services they are satisfied with very often.

On the other hand, if they answer the question by saying, "I need to have a personal experience before I ever make a referral to anybody else," then you have a benchmark for understanding their personal values.

You can then ask a follow-up question such as:

"Can you think of an example of a product or service that you have referred to someone, like a car, vacation spot, movie, restaurant?"

And then let them answer. If they give you an answer describing something they have referred to friends or family, ask them:

"What caused you to make the referral?"

Listen to their answer. At this point you will have developed a much higher level of confidence than most advisors have as you segue into the process of asking for a referral. You will also have identified any potential hot buttons or "land mines" involving referrals the client had given in the past that have blown up.

I find it interesting that many advisors who are supremely confident in so many other facets of their business all of a sudden become as awkward as a teenager on his first date when it comes to asking for a referral.

I have a strategy that is revolutionary in its simplicity that can help to reduce or eliminate much of the awkwardness typically associated with asking for a referral.

At the end of one of my client meetings, with a client in her early seventies, I said, "Irene, I have a very important question I would like to ask you. The reason I want to ask you this question is because I recently was referred to one of my client's sisters and her husband. At that meeting I discovered the husband was about to retire after 38 years working for the local newspaper. He was just about to make an irrevocable decision about which pension option he would select for the rest of his life. As a result of that conversation, I learned that he did not have anyone advising him on this important decision. I explained that I had helped almost 50 other people in the same situation to understand their options and make the best decision for their circumstances. I showed him how to take a different option than he was planning to select. This option would insure that his wife was protected if he died prematurely and would increase his monthly income by $1,200 for the rest of his life. If my client had not given me the referral, this couple would likely have made a decision that would have cost them tens of thousands of dollars and could not be changed. As a result of this experience, I have decided to ask you, and all my clients, to think about people you may know who are friends or family and might be a fit for what I do. I would like to show you this ideal client profile form I have developed, which *helps to clarify the kinds of people that can most benefit from what I do.* As you look at this form, is there anyone in any of these categories you can think of to whom you can recommend I send my client information kit? This kit explains how I help my clients achieve their financial goals."

Irene smiled and said, "Now that you mention it, my sister is retiring and she has been asking me for advice about what to do. I've mentioned what you do for me but she's never asked me for your number."

"Do you think it would be okay for me to give her a call directly?" I asked.

"Sure, I'll give you her number."

Irene had been a client for five years and I had never received a referral from her until I developed this approach.

What I did differently was tell a story to communicate an **idea** that helped change the context as to why I feel it is important to ask everyone for referrals, even though I don't expect everyone to become a great referral source.

Creating an Ideal Client Profile Form is extremely useful, because it helps remind people of connections they have that may be helpful to you. We are all trained to notice certain things. When you buy a new car, you begin to notice that kind of car on the road more often. It is not because there are more of them, you are just more aware of them. In the same way, you need to make sure your best referral clients know who you are looking for so that they will notice the people in their world who may be a match for you.

Your Ideal Client Profile, described in chapter 4, can be a paragraph or a series of bullet points created from your own database analysis. In my case, as you will recall, it was people who were 55 and older, who were retired or had recently received a buy-out package from an employer, owned their own small business, or were in the medical industry. By explaining what I was looking for, I improved my success ratio because my clients understood who I was looking for. This is the same concept as asking a friend for a restaurant referral in a new city. You need to explain whether you are looking for an elegant five-star dining experience or a local casual seafood restaurant. By clarifying your request, you increase the odds of receiving the information you are looking for.

You might be concerned that if you tell people specifically the type of person you are looking for, this will preclude them from telling you about a referral that doesn't fit your profile. You should explain that this is a general guideline to help them think about people they know who would be a fit for your services, but that there are, of course, exceptions to this profile.

By positioning your Ideal Client Profile this way, you get the benefit of having your referral source concentrate their attention on your best prospects while keeping the door open for any exception to the rule that might make sense. This approach allows you to ask additional questions about the referral prospect, and in most cases, you may still want to follow up with them anyway. Nevertheless, the perception is created that you work primarily with a select group of people who fit a certain profile. I have found this approach far more effective than just asking for names.

I believe this strategy is preferable to the script some advisors use, which says something like this: "I expect all my clients to help me grow my business, and the way you can do that, in addition to what you already pay me, is to provide me with referrals." I would find it hard to say this type of script with a straight face. It's not your client's responsibility to help you grow your business, but in many cases, they will do just that if asked properly.

Obviously you need to customize how to tell your "Irene Referral Story" so you can say it comfortably and in a way that makes sense for you.

"If you were me . . ."

One other script that can be very helpful in overcoming the inertia around asking for referrals is the phrase "If you were me . . . " This is the strategy I talked about in Chapter 4 for leveraging the seminar I presented to the employees of the state mental hospital that was closing.

After the seminar had been successfully completed, I said to the HR director, "Steve, if you were me, how would you go about duplicating what we have done here at the other hospitals that are preparing to close?"

He replied, "Well, now that you ask, I can refer you to some of the other hospital directors. In fact, I can even write you a letter of recommendation that you can use to introduce yourself to my colleagues."

As you can see, there is no one correct way to ask for referrals. But having a proven strategy in place is far more effective than making it up as you go along. It is also imperative to know that for some people it makes sense to back off rather than risk being too aggressive and annoying them. It is important to be aware of any resistance you receive and to recognize that there is probably a good reason for it.

Sometimes the best strategy is simply to ask for a letter of recommendation. This serves as a public commitment to the value you provide, and allows you to revisit the subject of referrals at your next meeting. Wealthy clients have confirmed in several major studies that referrals are their number-one source for finding a new advisor, so mastering this skill can have a direct impact on your business.

It's the little things that make a big difference

Some of the most successful companies today have developed a process that turns their customers and clients into "raving fans." Here's a quick example:

A friend of mine dropped his wife's watch off at Nordstrom's to have the battery replaced. The sales clerk, who remembered him from when he purchased the watch, told him the battery would be replaced within an hour. When he returned, my friend asked what the charge would be. She handed him the watch back and said that there was no charge for a Nordstrom's customer. The $10 that Nordstrom might have charged has paid the company far more in terms of referrals and good will.

How can you apply this concept as a financial advisor? The overriding referral principle is anticipating your clients' needs and exceeding their expectations. This is your best and least expensive form of advertising.

The EZ referral

An advisor named John recently told me about an example of his exceptional client service. John had a 7:00 a.m. meeting with a client in downtown New York City. The client arrived 20 minutes late and was very frustrated because he had been stuck in traffic at a toll booth outside the city. John asked him if he was familiar with the EZ Pass, a device that automatically collects your toll as you roll through a special toll booth. His client said he had always meant to get an EZ Pass but had simply been too busy. John said, "I'm going to fax you a form when you get to your office today and solve this problem for you." The client smiled and said, "If you say so." Two hours later, John's assistant faxed the application form for EZ Pass and linked it to the client's money market account, from which the toll charges would be withdrawn. A week later, John received a phone call from his EZ Pass client, thanking him for taking care of this and asking him if he would do the same for his client's wife. This client was more appreciative of this small personal gesture than he had been of many other seemingly more important business matters. Best of all, when John held a wine-tasting client appreciation event for about 20 clients and their guests, his EZ Pass client was very happy to recount what John had done for him above and beyond his normal role as a financial advisor. He paid John a huge compliment in front of many of his other best clients—and some prospects—by saying, "What I like most about John is that I really feel he looks out for me and my family's best interests."

A well-orchestrated client appreciation event can be the perfect forum for you to position yourself as a trusted advisor who makes a difference in your clients' lives. This only happens when you really *do* go the extra mile for your clients.

A word of warning

Most people have had the experience of making a referral that backfired. I have a friend, Jane, who was referred to a financial advisor by her sister-in-law, who had worked with this advisor for several years. The sister-in-law had been very happy with the advisor. About three months after Jane started working with this advisor, she discovered that he was doing something with her account that she deemed unethical. As a result she fired the advisor. The advisor then called the sister-in-law and told her that Jane was irrational and had accused him of unethical activities for which he said he was blameless. This caused such a rift between Jane and her sister-in-law that they did not speak for more than a year, because the sister-in-law sided with the advisor.

The reason I tell you this story is because it is important to remember that when somebody gives you a referral, they are going out on a limb for you by assuming some risk, and this gesture must not be taken lightly. I believe the referral process should be approached with respect and not be presented to clients in such a way that presumes that the advisor is owed the referral.

Referral etiquette

We've all heard the Aesop's fable of the man who killed the goose that laid the golden eggs. The biggest mistake I have seen in the referral process is the final step, which is forgetting to call the person who gave you the referral to thank them and tell them what happened with the lead the person gave you.

Make no mistake: People want to know whether the referral was successful or not, and it is a sign of respect to follow up and tell them whether you have met with the person and where things stand. Even if the referral was not successful, tell them what happened and let them know how much you appreciate their willingness to help you. Gratitude for the referrals you have already been given is often the key ingredient that keeps the referral stream flowing. How do you express that gratitude? I have seen many different approaches used, from a simple thank-you card to a phone call, personal visit or appropriate gift.

These small steps are the key to your ensuring that clients will want to give you more referrals because you have proven to be reliable, kept your promises to them, treated them with respect, and stayed in touch with them through good times and bad.

Always remember to treat your referral sources as the **golden goose** of your business.

Take Away Lessons

- **The most profitable way to grow your business is to get referrals**. This can be the start of your new marketing effort.
- **How do you get referrals?** You ask satisfied clients for them, pointing out that you hope to help the person you are referred to as much as you helped your client.
- **Clients don't owe you a referral**. If they don't want to give you one, don't insist.
- **Follow up.** Always let the person who gave you a referral know the outcome of the meeting.

"A good name, like good will, is made by many actions and may be lost by one"
Lord Jeffrey

Knowledge Application

1. Review your ideal client profile and list the five clients who have given you the most valuable referrals.

2. Practice the Referability Test questions so you can ask them comfortably.

3. Create a referral story to use as part of your presentation.

4. Determine the steps of your referral process, placing special emphasis on how you show your gratitude to those who have referred you.

5. Think about people you have referred to your friends and family and why you referred them. Then think about people you wouldn't refer and why.

Chapter 7

Your Marching Orders

How to get there from here.

What's ahead in this chapter

We will touch briefly on the key lessons in the book, and give you your marching orders to help you apply what you have learned so that you can maximize your personal return on investment.

Ambitious plans

I'll admit I had a pretty ambitious objective when I sat down and began writing **The Product is You.** I had three specific goals:
1. Capture all the best ideas I have heard working with top performing advisors.
2. Get down on paper all the "best practices" I had learned (often the hard way) in my years in the business.
3. Figure out a way to bring the human part of all of us back into the sales process.

So much time and money is spent teaching advisors technical matters (the in and outs of the products they are selling) and tactical issues (the best way to close a sale), that what makes each of us unique is often left out of the process.

But I have learned that the very best performers are not only outstanding on both the technical and tactical, they are also authentic to who they are. In fact, they have realized that above all else, the product they are selling first and foremost is themselves.

Taking stock of *you*

In the retail world, storeowners need to take stock to determine what has been selling and what has been left on the shelf. In the same way, now is the time for you to take stock of your current situation and determine what you need to do to grow your business.

However, as you know, it is very difficult to see our own blind spots.

I have worked hard to develop the ability to quickly assess and take stock of my coaching clients' financial advisory businesses.

I have been referred to a number of advisors who tell me that they know what to do intellectually to grow their business, but they get overwhelmed trying to implement new strategies because they don't know where to begin.

As my coaching clients have moved through the process outlined in this book, I have discovered that one of the most important facets of what I do is to break the process down into segments they can accomplish in 30-day segments.

Your marching orders upon completion of this book are to complete each of the steps below in 30-day segments. The most effective way to do this is to block off a half day *out of the office* where you will not be distracted, and complete each step. I recommend you complete the steps in the order listed. (If you have already accomplished one or more of the steps, so much the better.)

1. **Determine your mental thermostat level** by answering the questions at the end of chapter one. This will help you understand what truly motivates you.

2. **Create a Personal Biography**. Make sure it clearly explains to clients who you are and why you can help them. You can, and should, create different biographies depending on whom you will be

meeting with. The sample questions in Chapter Two will help you get started.

3. **Determine why you add value**. You need to know—and be able to communicate—why someone should do business with you rather than a competitor.

4. **Create a compelling elevator story.** Rehearse it so well that you can do it in your sleep. Once you have the basic speech down, create separate ones for different situations. You will find examples in Chapter 3.

5. **Fish where the fish are.** Vow to spend almost all of your time calling on your best prospects. Your to-do step here is to figure out who those best prospects are. Fill out your Ideal Client Profile Form covered in Chapter 4.

6. **Put your IPO Kit together.** Encapsulate the essence of who you are and what you do in a way that is easy to understand and distribute. You will see samples in Chapter 5.

7. **Leverage your best relationships**. Having identified your best prospects, ask for referrals, concentrating on trying to get people just like them. Review Chapter 6 for specific strategies.

To assist you in applying what you have learned in a systematic fashion, I suggest you visit www.productisyou.com to view specific examples of how other top performers have applied the concepts in this book.

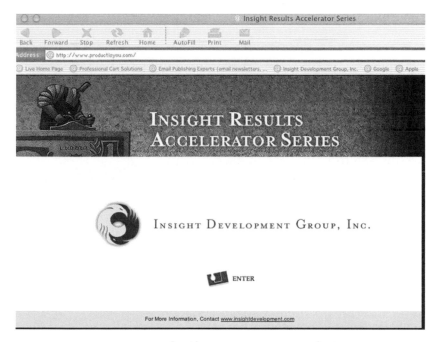

www.productisyou.com screen shot

The story below, based on the real-life experience of a financial advisor client of mine whom I'll call John, ties together all the concepts we have talked about so far.

The $500 million dollar man

John opened the newspaper one day and saw a headline that caught his eye: A local company had just been purchased for more than $1 billion. Bob, the president of the company, had been a client of John's for the past five years. During that time, Jim, the company's owner, had promoted Bob to the role of president. Jim would earn just over $1 billion from the sale of his company.

John called Bob to congratulate him about this exciting development. The conversation didn't go exactly as he had planned.

"John, I am glad you called," Bob said. "I want to talk to you."

Hearing his tone, John knew there was a problem.

John suggested that they meet in person, which they did a few days later. At the meeting, Bob told John that he appreciated all the hard work he had done over the past five years as his financial advisor. However, as a result of the buyout, he was now in a different financial category—he would be receiving several million dollars as part of the buyout—and he just didn't believe that John's firm had sufficient resources to advise him in his new financial status.

John was taken aback. A turn of events that had seemed so promising for him—a client coming into a windfall—was on the verge of evaporating in front of his eyes.

But because Bob had a perception that John was qualified to manage up to $1 million, Bob believed he lacked the expertise to compete in the multi-million dollar arena.

John said, "Before you make a decision to leave our firm, I would like the opportunity to make a presentation to you, and I would appreciate your referral to Jim to make a presentation to him as well."

Bob reluctantly agreed, and they set a date.

John called one of his firm's high-net-worth specialists to help make this important presentation. The specialist insisted on running the meeting, and that he would bring the presentation for the client.

At 7:30 a.m. on the day of the presentation, the specialist called John to say he wouldn't be able to make the meeting—all planes had been grounded due to weather—but he would be happy to e-mail the presentation for John to do himself.

John had only two hours to work with his assistant to try to put the presentation together. He knew it was unlikely that he was going to save the account because he lacked the time to prepare sufficiently to make a positive impression.

The meeting began, and it was soon apparent that John was not prepared. The result: Bob's concerns about John's firm not being up to the task of handling high-net-worth clients were validated.

At the end of the meeting, Bob said he appreciated everything John had done up to this point, but that he still wanted to transfer his money to a more specialized boutique firm. John told him he understood and that he would get it taken care of.

John ended the meeting by saying, "Bob, I know this presentation didn't go well and you know this is not representative of what normally happens when working with me. Therefore, I would like to ask you, '**If you were me**, how would you approach Jim to ask for a chance to present for his account. I intend to put together a team that includes the best of the best at my firm to avoid a repeat of today and demonstrate our true capabilities.'

Impressed by John's candor, Bob said, "I will make the introduction, but after that, it's up to you."

After the crushing defeat he had just experienced, John decided he needed to change his strategy if he was going to have any hope of closing a $1 billion deal with Jim.

John spoke with a few senior executives at his firm who suggested he should partner with another advisor who specialized in working with high-net-worth clients and had developed a reputation in this arena.

John met with Frank, the high-net-worth advisor, who told him that one thing he had learned in dealing with high-net-worth clients was that it is important not only to have the right members of the team in place but to demonstrate that each member of the team is an expert in his or her respective area.

Frank insisted that they plan out each facet of their presentation using a detailed script. From his past experience, Frank already knew the most likely questions they would be asked, and he had developed his own powerful way to answer them.

Frank told John that he needed his personal biography because they were preparing a combined team biography that would be presented to the prospective client with the proposal. Up until this point, John did not use a personal biography. Nor had he prepared a carefully thought-out script to answer the most likely objections.

The day of the big presentation arrived, and all of their rehearsal and preparation paid off. After flawlessly transitioning from one team member to the other, Frank summarized the investment services being offered and asked Jim and his investment committee if there were any questions. The business owner looked to his advisors in the room, including his former president, Bob. They began asking a series of questions. Frank answered them as elegantly and effortlessly as a professional tennis player returning lobs from a rookie. He had a well-prepared answer for almost every question they asked, because he had anticipated the most likely questions. However, he answered the questions so naturally that no one realized it had been scripted. As the meeting concluded, Bob said to John, "Well done."

One week later, John received a phone call from Bob, who said, "I've got good news and bad news. The bad news is that you didn't get all of Jim's money, but the good news is you are getting half." Then Bob said, "I never knew that you had so many talented people as part of your team, and I've decided that I'm moving my account back to you."

John was amazed at how this turnaround had occurred. He was incredibly pleased to have developed one of the largest consulting relationships at his firm, with just over $500 million. And with Bob's return as a client, he felt a sense of redemption. As a result of this experience, Bob had a new perception of John's capabilities as an advisor and his firm's capability as a money manager.

Success leaves clues

What this story demonstrated to me is that **success leaves clues.** There is a specific set of strategies and tactics that the most successful advisors use.

What you will notice in reading this story is that John and his team used almost all of the concepts I have covered in this book. John paid attention to Bob's **tonality** when he first called and said he wanted to meet. In the process of winning this business, John's team used **personal and team biographies** to help credentialize themselves. They developed and rehearsed a specific **Elevator Speech** to explain their value proposition. John transformed his **psychic real estate** in the mind of his client, Bob, by demonstrating his true capabilities. John and Frank worked together in a strategic partnership to win an account that John would have been unlikely to win on his own.

Best of all, the opportunity to win this $500 million deal all began with asking for a referral. Six months into their new relationship, during their second client review, John asked Bob for his assistance in referring John to other billion-dollar accounts. Bob said "I'm impressed with what you have done so far, for me personally and with Jim's portfolio, and I have a few ideas for you on how to develop other large relationships like Jim." Bob then recommended an association that included several other family offices like Jim's. This was something John never even knew existed, and he realized that this would be a great way to "fish where the fish are."

It's been said that irony is the driving force in the universe. Bob first became John's client as a result of a cold call made five years earlier with an offer of municipal bonds. This underscores that no matter how sophisticated your marketing process becomes, never underestimate the power of making one more call.

The closing bell

Now that you're armed with all that you have learned or rediscovered in this book, what are you going to do with it? Are you going to say, "That was interesting," and put the book back on the shelf? Or has what you have learned helped to reset your Mental Thermostat to expand what you believe you are capable of achieving. Remember that one degree can make a tremendous difference. If it can transform water into steam, inaction into action, then it can transform a commodity into a highly valued product—**YOU.**

Let me end with a story.

A long time ago, there were two great orators of antiquity who spoke to a large crowd. When Cicero finished his speech, the crowd stood up and politely applauded. But, when Demosthenes finished his speech, the crowd, moved to action, stood up and shouted, **"Let us march."**

My goal in writing this book is not to receive polite applause but rather to get you to take away at least one idea that will compel you to stand up and march. I wish you much success on your journey.

"It's what you learn after you know it all that counts"
John Wooden

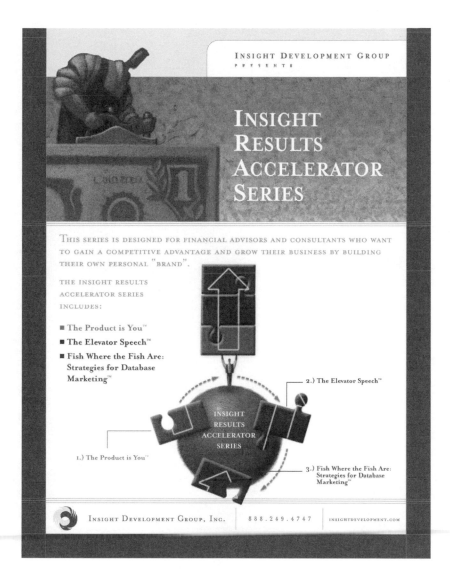

For more information on Mark's programs or products, visit
www.productisyou.com or call 888-249-4747

INSIGHT RESULTS ACCELERATOR SERIES

The Product is You™

In this dynamic session, you will learn the importance of the impression you leave in the mind of your prospects and clients. You will also learn how to position yourself as an expert in your field with a biography and letters of recommendation. This session includes a breakout segment where you will learn how to effectively generate referrals using your new collateral material.

Benefit to You: The written questionnaire to create your biography and samples for you to model.

The Elevator Speech™

Have you ever been asked "What do you do?" and responded in a way that you knew the other person really didn't understand? During this dynamic workshop, you will learn how to quickly and effectively communicate what you do in the form of an "elevator speech".

Benefit to You: A written "elevator speech" that you can begin using with your clients and prospects immediately.

Fish Where the Fish Are: Strategies for Database Marketing™

In this highly interactive program, you will learn how to effectively use your database to create "Business Intelligence" using the metaphor of a Fish Finder. Just as a Fish Finder enables a fisherman to see where the fish are and what strategy he should use to catch them, you will learn how to apply this idea to your business. This new way of discerning information from your database will allow you to see patterns and connections that were previously invisible.

Benefit to You: Identifying your ideal target client and the best strategy to attract them.

Mark Magnacca is the President of Insight Development Group. He is an internationally recognized peak performance strategist and sales coach whose mission is to help his clients boost their performance to a higher level of achievement.

Mark developed the content for "The Results Accelerator Series" while building his own financial advisory business from 1988 to 1998.

Using these strategies he was consistently ranked among the top producers in the financial services industry.

Mark's seminar programs have been utilized by many leading firms which include Merrill Lynch, INVESCO, Metlife and Commonwealth Financial Network.

His programs have been featured in The New York Times, USA Today, The Wall Street Journal and on CNN's Money Line with Lou Dobbs.

INSIGHT DEVELOPMENT GROUP, INC. 888.249.4747 INSIGHTDEVELOPMENT.COM

About the Author

Mark Magnacca, is the president of Insight Development Group. He is a nationally recognized speaker, creative marketing specialist, and sales coach whose mission is to help his clients boost their performance to a higher level of achievement.

His turnkey process known as C.A.L.M. helps his clients to Create a compelling message, Articulate that message effectively, Locate their target market, and Motivate them to take action.

While building his own financial advisory firm, he was responsible for creating and implementing innovative business building strategies. These strategies have become the foundation for The Product is You.

Mark has presented his training programs for many leading financial firms, which include Merrill Lynch, Smith Barney, Fidelity and MetLife.

Mark's programs have been featured in both print and television media including The New York Times, The Wall Street Journal, Registered Rep, Financial Planning and CNN's Money Line.